PROPHETS OF FREEDOM AND ENTERPRISE

PROPHETS OF FREEDOM AND ENTERPRISE

Essays by Antony Flew, Malcolm Hoppe, A. R. Ilersic, Michael Jefferson, Wilfrid Sendall, Alfred Sherman, Alan Walters, Peregrine Worsthorne

Edited by Michael Ivens

KOGAN PAGE
for
AIMS OF INDUSTRY

First published 1975
by Kogan Page Ltd.
116a Pentonville Road, London N.1
for Aims of Industry

Printed in Great Britain
by W & J Mackay Limited
Chatham

ISBN 0 85038 241 6

CONTENTS

INTRODUCTION – THE FREEDOMS

MICHAEL IVENS

That a free society and a free economy go together has been brought home to many of us as totalitarian States have simultaneously destroyed both. We have also seen how attacks on liberal economies by interventionist governments have damaged political, cultural and individual freedoms. These days then we must agree with Marx that the nature of the economy affects values. But then we must stand him on his head and go on to say that Marx drew the wrong conclusions. A liberal economy is essential to personal and cultural freedom.

This collection of essays on 'Prophets of Freedom and Enterprise' is by a number of distinguished writers. It assesses the significance today of some of the great thinkers whose works have revealed not merely economic truths, but also the need for individual and group freedoms.

Selecting the thinkers for exploration was not easy: clearly we could have also included David Hume, Bentham, Ricardo, Locke, von Humboldt, Lord Acton, Milton, Goethe, Erasmus, de Tocqueville and Whitman. Not all of these may have been economists but all were strong on freedom.

Adam Smith provides our first great example of the many-sided thinker: economist, philosopher and sociologist. As Alfred Sherman points out in his brilliant essay, Smith, like Marx, has not always been lucky in his disciples. Nor for that matter, echoes Malcolm Hoppe, has Keynes.

Marx, with his strong Judaic sense of the culminating Day of the Lord thought that historical processes would destroy capitalism. Lenin, however, realized brilliantly that determined and thorough organization could transform an under-developed country into a shattering force.

Neither could have dreamed, as Professor Sutton has shown, that Western capitalism would have cheerfully contributed 90% of the Soviet technology – very often at knock-down prices subsidised by the taxpayer. Russian astronauts stepping out in American spacesuits would have appealed to Lenin's grim humour.

The veritable confusion of our times makes it important that those who oppose the drift to authoritarianism and corporatism, whether through their work or their thought, must be clear in their principles and philosophies. Too often liberals, conservatives and non-political entrepreneurs are sounder on practice than on philosophy.

It is not sufficient to be merely in favour of freedom. We must understand the inter-dependence of the great subjects of debate: economics, politics, philosophy and sociology. That is why Adam Smith, with his strong emphasis on the inter-dependence of disciplines – and incidentally of people – is such a natural first subject.

Smith tends to be known only too often by a swift and vague reference to his 'Invisible Hand', and a conviction that he believed in work specialization – particularly with regard to pins. In fact Adam Smith was opposed to an excessive division of labour and believed that it could wreck society. He approved of certain Government roles and he would have approved of the recent American creative work programme. On the other hand, he knew only too well that private prodigality could lead to work for many whereas public prodigality could damage society.

The greatest challenge today, as Alfred Sherman points out, is to find an alternative to the Puritan work ethic which appealed to Adam Smith.

Professor Flew is one of those rare beings who can ride the mounts of philosophy and economics at the same time, and he meets head-on the charge that John Stuart Mill was a socialist. This collection has not gone for identity of views in subject or authors; Popper, who is sceptical of those who prescribe happiness for others, is challenging to Mill on this and also on his historicism. And, as Professor Ilersic records, Marshall was influenced towards socialist thought at one time by Mill.

In these blurred days, Marshall provides welcome classical realism. He was one of those rare economists who went and looked at industry and the workers face-to-face. As Professor Ilersic points out, Marshall noted that trade unionists were tempted to death-wishes of restrictive practices and restrictive labour, which could destroy their own employment. Britain is experiencing this, and Fleet Street illustrates Marshall's dictum on restricting labour in the trade.

Marshall above all points the moral: forget economic forces at your peril.

Inflation in the Western world has led to an interest in the so-called monetarists such as Milton Friedman. Both von Mises and Friedman have also increasingly written on freedom and those who threaten it. Professor Friedman has shown brilliantly the dangers of created-inflation, but has also illustrated how a liberal economy can protect those who are persecuted by illiberalism; he chose the victims of McCarthyism as an example of those who fly to free enterprise for succour. Nor has Professor Friedman made too many friends in official quarters by showing that the poor could have done better without poverty programmes.

Like Milton Friedman, Ludwig von Mises has come to contemplate "*les trahisons des clercs*". The anti-capitalist mentality, as von Mises has termed it, is something that bears considerable reflection. Many of those intellectuals who call for the destruction of moral frontiers are often those who are most impatient of the freedom to set up businesses, to manufacture, sell, and re-invest.

Although we may grow pessimistic at the swing to intolerance and extremism of intellectuals during this century we should, on the other hand, take some consolation in Professor Walter's point that it is astonishing to find so many conscientious workers who resist temptations that the State provides to lure them to paid unemployment or paid strikes.

Keynes is glorified as the destroyer of cyclical demons and mass unemployment, while at the same time he is accused of being the creator of international inflation. Malcom Hoppe lays much blame on his disciples, and Hayek also shares this view. In Britain, where lack of labour mobility and its encouragement has caused so much damage, we would be wise to go back to Keynes' distinction between lack of mobility and involuntary unemployment.

In the Western world, capitalism tends to be attacked by its opponents on moral, social and political grounds. As the defenders lob back economic arguments neither side communicates. It is vital that the thinkers of the free society should offer vision and nobility, and Popper and Hayek are excellent 'prophets' with whom to finish, even though both are suspicious of prophecy.

Wilfrid Sendall's study of Popper is notable for an interesting line of argument – that the growth of trade in Britain, Holland and Belgium influenced the birth of democracy. Popper himself manages to communicate a grand vision of the Open Society while disposing of its enemies from Plato onwards.

Popper, in the *Open Society*, is (like Alfred Sherman in his present contribution) more generous to Marx than some of us might be. Hayek was forthright in his warnings of the Servile State which is beginning to envelope us. Winston Churchill, impressed by Hayek, telescoped time and attacked Attlee and the post-war Labour Party as being likely to lead to national socialism. He was too early and the public were unconvinced.

Thirty years later in Britain, a deluge of economic measures which would not have called for comment in Mussolini's Italy are now upon us. You can be too soon . . .

In the United States, however, Hayek is increasing in influence and in Britain he is quoted by Mrs Margaret Thatcher and Sir Keith Joseph.

Hayek is also all-too relevant on the importance of law. The United States stumbles because Presidents and others break the law. Britain moves towards confusion because the trade unions overthrow law by force.

Hayek's *Constitution of Liberty* is a magnificent edifice. As Worsthorne points out, Hayek has confronted many of the problems of our time and given heartening answers. Dealing with the threat to law by the trade unions – and others – would provide a splendid roof on his great construction.

Time, of course, is not on the side of the economic and cultural liberals. The tide away from liberalism has to be turned back, and as Hayek says, it must not be done in the interests of just one particular class or group. But there is no retreating. As Popper states: 'If we wish to remain human, then there is only one way, the way into the open society'.

RESTORING ADAM SMITH

ALFRED SHERMAN

An essay on Adam Smith starts out with a dilemma. Smith has paid the penalty for greatness by becoming known to millions at second, third and fourth hand, becoming staler with each transaction. The essayist setting out to restore Smith will be strongly tempted to offer an alternative resumé of what Smith really meant. Had Smith, who was a master of language, considered his ideas reducible to a couple of hundred sentences, the length of this tribute, he would have written it himself. He did not, so neither shall I.

The essayist's job is to restore the father of political economy's own work by removing the deposits of misunderstanding and misinterpretation which have accreted during two centuries from the fall-out of our intellectual climate. When the scale is chipped away from *The Wealth of Nations*, the lines of its thought stand out for themselves. If the essayist has done his job aright, those who have not read Smith at first hand will be encouraged to do so, those who have will draw on it for inspiration in the never-ending struggle against artery-clogging encroachment by political power on economic process.

The key to Smith's work, the misunderstandings and misinterpretations of it, and his influence, in its high tide and ebb, lies with his 'invisible hand'. First his would-be disciples misunderstood it; then their misunderstanding paved the way for misrepresentation by those who would control us in one way or another.

Smith's 'invisible hand' was neither fatalistic nor optimistic; it did not argue that all would be for the best in the best of all possible worlds if only we left the hidden hand to operate freely. Nor did he regard self-interest as a sufficient guarantee of good. He was far too subtle, enlightened, sceptical and aware that history had many surprises in store. His thesis was that the great sweep of history, centuries of economic and political progress, had not come about as a result of the premeditated design of rulers, but as though by an invisible hand; as a result of great politico-economic forces generated by the interplay of millions on millions of people going about their affairs guided by a combination of self-interest, fellow-feeling and natural sympathy for other human beings, loyalties, concern for justice (itself motivated in good part by enlightened self-interest) and the wish to deserve to be well thought of. He gave a sense of the power of millions of people going about their own business and the short-sightedness of those who would manipulate national economies.

The Wealth of Nations traced the way in which economic and political change had interacted, and was continuing to interact. Smith did not ascribe any special moral virtue to self-interest or the desire to accumulate material wealth, as he did to more exalted emotions. He traced how men as they really were, with all their selfishness and imperfections, could nevertheless create just progressive societies. He argued that the best society was the one which could harness man's self-interest to wider social ends. He found that market-oriented societies did this, given certain provisos.

Smith is invariably compared with Marx; we might contrast their different approaches to human nature.

Smith took it for granted that if he was to write about society, he needed some theory of human nature, which he had elaborated as philosopher. He did not hold human nature to be static, nor did he speculate unduly about the limits to its possible change. He produced a working model of human nature and asked what kind of society best accommodated it, while not ignoring that society itself modified human behaviour.

Marx, by contrast, avoided adducing any explicit or consistent theory of human nature at all. He drew out of his Hegelian hat the idea that man's consciousness is conditioned – or determined, the pundits differ – by his environment. This sounds quite sophisticated until you ask what it really means: what it tells you about actual people's behaviour under given circumstances; what is incidental and what is unchangeably human. In practice, Marx avoided saying what he meant. Socialists have followed him in this, their implicit theories of human behaviour oscillating unpredictably between ascribing utter hedonism, utter selflessness and 'class-conditioning'. Marx toyed with an interpretation of the idea of 'false consciousness' (which is useful enough in itself if used with extreme caution) which posited that men act according to their class conditioning, not consciously, but moved, as it were, by an 'invisible brain'. But of course this metaphysical concept is useless as a tool of analysis to explain particular behaviour, not least because the working class never behaves as Marxists would like it to.

Since human nature is visibly a thorn in socialist flesh, it is worth going back to Smith, whose theories played so formative a part in British history for the next century, for a serviceable theory to underpin a free economy in a free society where men think for themselves. The difference in the two thinkers' approach to human nature exemplifies a wider distinction between them. Marx mixed up his role as analyst with prophet and 'legislator for mankind'. He never chose to differentiate between predictions and prescriptions, between what he thought inevitable and what desirable. Worse still, he violated his own dialectic when he posited a socialist nirvana beyond the last antithesis, when contradictions would come to an end. They never will!

Adam Smith presumed less. He avoided moralising, confident that his readers were just as capable as he was of drawing moral implications. He did not predict a free-market utopia just beyond the rainbow. On the contrary, he was a truer dialectician than either Marx or Hegel, precisely because of his empirical and sceptical approach. For example, after demonstrating the vital function performed by division of labour as an engine of economic progress, he then speculated that if carried to its logical conclusion it could wreak havoc on society. It would bring 'mental mutilation' to the workers, he argued, stultifying them, and thereby adversely affecting them as people and as citizens, making them easy meat for demagogues and panacea-mongers. He did not propose any certain remedy for this eventuality, preferring to leave something for posterity to solve; but he did insist that this was a matter to which government should address itself seriously.

For, contrary to the widely-held image, Smith did not wish to exclude government to the margins of society. He saw a great role for it, but primarily in creating the framework within which people of all classes could get about their business, which is more than it has done so far. He drew many examples of economies' failure to develop because those in power consumed the whole surplus which would otherwise have been devoted to investment.

> 'Great nations are never impoverished by private, though they sometimes are by public prodigality and misconduct. The whole, or almost the whole public revenue, is in most countries employed in maintaining unproductive hands . . . Those unproductive hands, who should be maintained by a part only of the spare revenue of the people, may consume so great a share of their whole revenue, and thereby oblige so great a number to encroach upon their capitals, upon the funds destined for the maintenance of productive labour, that all the frugality and good conduct of individuals may not be able to compensate the waste and degradation of produce occasioned by this violent and forced encroachment.'

He could not have foreseen that the day would come when, in addition to economic loss due to 'public prodigality,' governments would also waste much of the substance of the nation in subsidies to economically-inefficient enterprises, that 'prodigal production' would be added to forms of intervention already known to him.

Of course, he was well aware of the propensity of vested interests to seek protection or other forms of monopoly and of governments to grant them. (He did not foresee the day when the workers, with whom he sympathised so strongly, would join in this conspiracy against the public good, their own at one remove.) But he lived at a time of increasing economic rationality, which his own writings enormously advanced. We live in a period of regression from rationality; it would be unfair to Smith to go to his writings for light on the causes of this retrogression, though some of his warnings were relevant. (They include the observation that free training for professional and academic occupations would influence both remuneration and quality – small wonder that this intellectual proletariat lends its weight to further State takeover.)

When Smith wrote, his ideas had immediate and beneficial but one-sided impact. Many obstacles to economic growth were swept away. It was Adam Smith's Britain which led the world for several generations. But with economic progress, new problems emerged, which needed new thinking, new Adam Smiths. In the hands of lesser men – better economists than political economists – his ideas were turned into dogma and apologetics; the vacuum came to be filled by the false prophets.

Characteristically, Marx himself never blamed Smith for his *epigoni*, but wrote of Smith, whom he extensively drew on, with great respect. But, then, Marx was to have even less luck with his own posthumous followers.

I stress the distinction between economists and political economists. Smith was a philosopher and what we would properly call a sociologist. He came to economics from outside, having made his name elsewhere, and saw economic theory as part of a wider whole. He would never have dreamed of trying to abstract economic activity from its socio-political context, or of confusing wealth with wellbeing. He saw progress not only in terms of increasing wealth, but also of wider freedom, of the enhanced right of men to choose their occupation and take their future in their own hands. The history of over a thousand years of progress, as he recorded it, presented material wellbeing, freedom, justice and security as inextricably interrelated. His mistrust of governments led him to the conviction that the true greatness of the free economy, as he saw it emerging in his corner of the world, was that it automatically disciplined people's striving for their own good and their families into serving their fellow-men. Two hundred years' subsequent experience, not the least the past thirty, has confirmed how right he was.

This stress on his political and sociological vision may seem one-sided to those brought up to admire his great economic tableau, that great intellectual structure adducing for the first time the working of a modern economy, which all subsequent economic theory has done little more than modify, and which was to influence thought and policy in half the world. But Smith never for one moment ceased to be aware that economics meant people, that an economy could never operate independently of the people who operated it, that if people did not work, the economy would not work, that laws, attitudes, propensity to save and to take risks and the ability to keep government rapacity in check, were all part of the social framework within which an economy functioned. He could not have comprehended the living economy had he not been guided by a philosophy of human endeavour.

Those of us who are proud to consider ourselves heirs of Adam Smith stand in greatest need of this aspect of his philosophy, if we are to win back widespread and popular acceptance for the enduring values of his economic approach. Man does not live by bread alone; he must feel that what he is doing is right and has wider meaning. Smith's great discoveries coincided with a religious and philosophical climate which valued personal endeavour highly, not because it valued the nation and other collective entities any less, but more because it could take them for granted.

We can no longer do so. If we are to restore the popular appreciation of the role of enterprise and the market which was created by Adam Smith two centuries ago, we must find the appropriate moral context and content. Efficiency, the market, utility, are all very well as tools of analysis, but no one will man the barricades in their name. We need human ideals for the market to serve. Insofar as we offer ideals which the market and free enterprise are alone capable of realizing, we create a more propitious climate for the economic logic we inherited from Smith.

In one sense, we are better placed than he was: we have a wealth of accumulated data on the bitter fruits of interference, the counter-productive effects which often weigh most heavily on the poorest as well as the most deserving, which intensify social tensions and political asperity. Experience of social relations in an economy where market and market-related sanctions have been largely neutralized may create greater readiness to appreciate some structure within which private and public good are harmonized by impersonal forces. The way will have been paved by disillusion with the fruits of tripartite meetings in Downing Street which blur the separate functions of government, industry and the trade unions (the last who by the nature of their profession ask and do not give). Which is where Adam Smith came in two centuries ago.

It is up to us, particularly those of us who sport an Adam Smith tie. In the perspective of 200 years, when we know that he succeeded, his task may seem easier than ours. But this is an optical illusion. Then, as now, there was an army of vested interests bred by controls; there were the philistines who said that if the government – and other governments, too – did it, then it must be right; there were those who said that his thesis was too simple, or went too far, or that the public was not ready for it.

Adam Smith did not lack cause for exasperation; for example, there had been the financial scandals in Scotland when some banks expanded currency without backing, impelled by belief that it must be in Scotland's interests and would surely bring greater production and prosperity; of course, it brought bankruptcy. But in spite of ample cause for exasperation, he presented his message in calm measured style, nourished by faith in the educated public's wisdom and ability to understand the truth persuasively presented. This is perhaps the most enduring part of his message. It is particularly relevant nowadays, when many of those who should have championed a free economy in a free society are all too ready to rationalise their irresolution by affecting to doubt the public's ability to appreciate the truth when it is told. Smith's success is an added encouragement to us to give the public the benefit of the doubt, and tell them the truth as we see it.

We can also be encouraged by his optimism regarding the great regenerative powers of a free or mainly free economy.

> 'The uniform, constant and uninterrupted effort of every man to better his condition, the principle from which public and national, as well as private opulence is originally derived, is frequently powerful enough to maintain the natural progress of things toward improvement, in spite both of the extravagance of government and of the greatest errors of administration. Like the unknown principle of animal life, it frequently restores health and vigour to the constitution, in spite not only of the disease, but of the absurd prescriptions of the doctor.'

True, government has grown larger and stronger than when he wrote. But so – I hope – have we. And, unlike him, we have giants like Adam Smith to draw inspiration from.

J. S. MILL: SOCIALIST OR LIBERTARIAN?

ANTONY FLEW

Some may wonder what John Stuart Mill is doing here. Surely Mill was eventually converted to a hesitant, deferred socialism? Certainly Mill himself wrote in his *Autobiography*, of the third period of his intellectual development, after he had come under the spell of Harriet Taylor: 'We were now much less democrats than I had been, because so long as education continues to be so wretchedly imperfect, we dreaded the ignorance and especially the selfishness and brutality of the mass: but our ideal of ultimate improvement went far beyond democracy, and would class us decidedly under the general designation of socialism'. He goes on: 'In the *Principles of Political Economy* these opinions were promulgated, less clearly and fully in the first edition, rather more so in the second, and quite unequivocally in the third'. Given so apparently straightforward and unambiguous a lead it is not surprising that in his Pelican Book on *John Stuart Mill* Karl Britton says: 'He later undertook a thorough examination of socialism in a work which occupied him during the last three years of his life. Four completed chapters were published in the *Fortnightly* in 1879, and constitute one of the foundations of Fabian socialism' (p. 43).

But now let us take a look at some of what Mill actually says in these two works. It will soon become clear that he would today be considerably more at home in the Selsdon Group than in the Fabian Society. The first relevant chapter of the *Principles* is that

"Of Property", where Mill prescribes that the word 'socialism' is to be 'applied to any system which requires that the land and the instruments of production should be the property, not of individuals, but of communities or associations, or of the government'. Although state ownership is thus specifically included within the meaning of the term, this chapter attends only to communities or associations. Mill's conclusions are anxious yet open-minded: 'It is yet to be ascertained', whether a scheme of common ownership of means of production combined with as near as makes little matter equal distribution of the product, 'would be consistent with that multiform development of human nature, those manifold unlikenesses, that diversity of tastes and talents, and variety of intellectual points of view, which not only form a great part of the interest of human life, but by bringing intellects into stimulating collision, and by presenting to each innumerable notions that he would not have conceived of himself, are the mainspring of mental and moral progression'. As for the much less drastically egalitarian schemes of Fourier and others, 'the thing to be desired, and to which they have a just claim, is opportunity of trial. They are all capable of being tried on a moderate scale, and at no risk, either personal or pecuniary, to any except those who try them'.

Sympathetic experimental interest in such cooperative enterprises, without state subsidies and presumably operating on equal terms against other competitors in a market, does not begin to make Mill even the grandfather of a Fabian socialist. On the contrary: David Alexander, a founder member of the Selsdon Group, recently suggested that if we ever do get a government persistently determined to turn back the tide of nationalization, one model for its hiving-off operations should be the National Industrial Fuel Efficiency Service. In its final year as a State operation it piled up a deficit of £67,500. It was bought, with the help of a £100,000 loan from Henry Ansbacher, by a private company formed by its employees. In 1973–4, its second year of operation, this private company made a profit of £28,429. (See *Yesterday, Today and Tomorrow* for November, 1974).

In the following chapter – "The Same Subject Continued" – Mill considers bequest and inheritance:

> 'The institution of property implies the power of bequest, but not the right of inheritance . . . Were I framing a code of law according to what seems to me best in itself . . . I should prefer to restrict, not what anyone might bequeath, but what anyone should be permitted to acquire by bequest . . . Each person should have power to dispose by will of his or her whole property; but not to lavish it in enriching some one individual, beyond a certain maximum, which should be fixed sufficiently high to afford the means of comfortable independence.'

In contemporary terms Mill would have welcomed an Accessions Tax, albeit with a much higher threshold than would be proposed by most advocates of such a tax in our time. He would even have been prepared for this tax to be progressive rather than proportionate; whereas he was utterly opposed to applying the progressive principle to the earnings or to savings from the earnings of the actual taxpayer[1]. But again this leaves Mill diametrically opposed to our socialists, even to the Manifesto 'moderates'. For they have all most deliberately chosen their Capital Transfer Tax rather than an Accessions Tax: precisely because the latter would tend to spread wealth more widely among the people; whereas the former must accelerate the desired concentration of all wealth and power into the hands of the State.

Mill returns to our present topics in Book IV of the *Principles* in a chapter "On the Probable Futurity of the Labouring Classes". Much of this deals with the pioneer cooperative in Rochdale, and with various enterprises in which most or all the workers have some sort of equity participation. Since there is no suggestion here of either monopoly or subsidy even the most austere of Selsdon Men could only smile approval. Before this chapter is through Mill will have us on our feet cheering. For it ends with a paean to competition. Mill sympathizes with such ventures in self-reliant participation and cooperation. But, he continues,

> 'I utterly dissent from the most conspicuous and vehement part of [socialist] teaching . . . declamations against competition . . . They forget that wherever competition is

not, monopoly is; and that monopoly, in all its forms, is the taxation of the industrious for the support of indolence, if not of plunder . . . I do not pretend that there are no inconveniences in competition . . . But if competition has its evils, it prevents greater evils . . . no one can foresee the time when it will not be indispensible to progress . . . every restriction of it is an evil, and every extension of it, even if for the time injuriously affecting some class of labourers, is always an ultimate good'.[2]

Benighted Victorian that he was Mill had never heard of, for instance, the latest plans to reduce the service at Felixstowe to the present London level by establishing a complete State ports monopoly. But in his chapter "Of the Grounds and Limits of the *Laissez-Faire* or Non-Interference Principle" he recommends 'a course so seldom resorted to by governments'. This is 'that of giving advice or promulgating information' or, while 'leaving individuals free to use their own means', establishing 'side by side with their arrangements an agency of its own for a like purpose'. Some of Mill's examples are painfully topical: 'There might be a post-office, without penalties against the conveyance of letters by other means . . . public hospitals, without any restriction upon private medical or surgical practice'.[3]

Indeed there might. But this is certainly not socialism as that word is understood in Britain today. Later in this chapter Mill emphasizes the non-economic objection to monopoly, especially State monopoly. 'Education', he argues, 'is one of those things which it is admissible in principle that a government should provide for the people'; and he proceeds to advocate 'pecuniary support to elementary schools' from the public purse. However, the future author of the classic statement *On Liberty* insists,

'It is not endurable that a government should . . . have a complete control over . . . education . . . To possess such control, and actually exert it, is to be despotic. A government which can mould . . . the people from their youth upwards, can do with them whatever it pleases.'

It is thus as sure as any such counterfactual hypothetical can ever be that if Mill were alive today he would be pushing for educational vouchers.

It is this unsleeping concern for human individuality and for personal liberty which guarantees that Mill could never have become a recruit to Fabian socialism, or any other socialism of monopoly State corporations. (To me one of the most sinister features of our time is that the devotees of such socialism appear to be increasingly attracted by exactly what Mill saw as menaces.) In Mill's last words on the subject – the brief, posthumous, and incomplete *Chapters on Socialism* – he has several things to say about economic practicalities. But the strongest emphasis is on the dangers of making all decisions collective and political.

Characteristically he sets out to provide a sober 'survey of the two rival theories, that of private property and that of socialism' (p. 709).[4] He starts by giving a good run in quotation, to "Socialist Objections to the Present Order of Society" (pp. 711–727). He then cools things a little by pointing to some of the 'ignorance of economic facts' which it distresses him to find even 'in the representations of the ablest and most candid socialists'. One item is Louis Blanc's '*baisse continue des salaires*' (p. 727); which is more familiar to later generations as one of those validly deduced false consequences which ought to discredit the political economy of Marx's *Capital*. Another item is the evergreen illusion that the redistribution of all private profit would make possible a financial leap forward for all but a tiny class of professional rentiers (p. 735).

What Mill wants is to test the rival theories 'on an experimental scale, by actual trial'; though he adds 'that the intellectual and moral grounds of socialism deserve the most attentive study, as affording in many cases the guiding principles of the improvements necessary to give the present economic system of society its best chance' (p. 736). But clearly these tests 'on an experimental scale' would again involve only the voluntary development of unsubsidized cooperatives and communes, operating within a free market framework. They constitute, therefore, new forms of private enterprise; and as such they are the very opposite of socialism in the modern British sense.

Piecemeal, tentative, experimental moves of this sort are one thing. The wholesale and – as a certain Manifesto threatens – irreversible transformation of an entire society is quite another. Mill does not even consider a fully socialist economy, whether that is supposed to be reached at a stroke by revolutionary violence or step by step through a series of peaceful parliamentary terms. He dismissed this as simply impossible:

> '. . . the very idea of conducting the whole industry of a country by direction from a single centre is . . . obviously chimerical . . . if the revolutionary socialists attained their immediate object, and actually had the whole property of the country at their disposal, they would find no other practicable mode of exercising their power over it than that of dividing it into portions, each to be made over to the administration of a small socialist community' (p. 748).

Lenin's Bolsheviks, and their many successors in other countries, have now proved Mill wrong on this point of practicability; although we should add that it has yet to be shown, and that it scarcely looks as if it is going to be shown, that a country so peculiarly dependent as ours upon the export of manufactures and of sophisticated services can even maintain its living standards under such a system. But the whole experience of the now numerous State socialist countries shows how right Mill was in his fundamental non-economic fears. Making money truly is, as the cynic said, a comparatively harmless occupation:

> 'When selfish ambition is excluded from the field . . . of riches and pecuniary interest, it would betake itself with greater intensity to the domain still open to it . . . the struggles for preeminence and for influence in the management would be of great bitterness when the personal passions, diverted from their ordinary channel, are driven to seek their principal gratification in that other direction' (pp. 744–745).

Believing that a centralized socialist State was impossible, Mill's still strong warnings refer only to smaller associations:

'. . . even the dissensions which might be expected would be a far less evil . . . than a delusive unanimity produced by the prostration of all individual opinion and wishes before the decree of the majority . . . private life would be brought in a most unexampled degree within the dominion of public authority, and there would be less scope for the development of individual character and individual preferences than has hitherto existed among the full citizens of any state belonging to the progressive branches of the human family' (pp. 745 and 746).

I conclude with a final quotation. This one comes not from Mill but from a document called *The Falsifiers of Scientific Communism*, issued in 1972 by the Institute of Marxism-Leninism in Moscow. This document sketches a programme for the seizure of total, irremovable power by Communist Parties following 'united front' or 'broad left' tactics. We should take these words to heart; as they have surely been taken to heart by M. Marchais in France, by Sr. Cunhal and his soldier allies in Portugal, and by too many of those who toiled to ensure that our Labour Party became committed to what the then shadow Chancellor welcomed at the 1973 conference as 'a massive extension of nationalization'. The Moscow statement reads: 'Having once acquired political power, the working class implements the liquidation of the private ownership of the means of production . . . As a result, under socialism, there remains no ground for the existence of any opposition parties counterbalancing the Communist Party' (*The Economist*, 17/VI/72, p. 23).

NOTES

1. We too rarely remember, as Hayek reminds us, that British income tax only began to be progressive in 1910 and the American in 1913 (*The Constitution of Liberty*, p. 310).

2. While I was writing this paper Mr Len Murray urged the British people to break the Treaty of Rome on the grounds that the EEC is an old-fashioned organization, devoted to the unBritish or at any rate unsocialist idea of competition. Surely there are some in this country, as well as many on the continent of Europe, who would be more impressed by criticism of the competitive ethos if it came from those who had shown that they could meet and beat their commercial competitors; just as I am myself more attentive to any objections to 'the examination system' which come from those – like Mr Murray himself – who have achieved first-class honours in the schools?

3. It is also topical to mention Mill's treatment of "Laws against Combinations of Workmen" in the previous chapter "Of Interferences of Government Grounded on Erroneous Theories". Of such laws he says, both 'the end and the means are alike odious'. But he was not speaking of laws to ensure the widest participation in honestly conducted union elections. Nor had it ever entered his head that State welfare benefits might be given as of right to both strikers and their families: 'As support from public charity would of course be refused to those who could get work and would not accept it, they would be thrown for support upon the trades union of which they were members . . .' As for the latest Shrewsbury Martyrs, Mill insisted that 'No severity, necessary to the purpose, is too great to be employed against attempts to compel workmen to join a union, or take part in a strike by threats of violence.'

4. The page references are to Volume V of the definitive Toronto University Press *Collected Works*. Elsewhere, since there are many available editions, I have employed edition-neutral methods of citation.

THE REAL ECONOMIC WORLD: THE RELEVANCE OF ALFRED MARSHALL

A. R. ILERSIC

Lord Rothschild, when head of Mr Heath's 'think tank', was tactless enought to observe in public that, if Britain's disappointing rate of economic growth persisted, then by the 1980s the people of Britain would become the 'peasants' of Europe. Nothing has happened since then to disprove that prediction.

The basic characteristic of peasant economies is the wasteful use of labour in what is usually little more than a subsistence agrarian economy. Such 'disguised' unemployment, as the economist describes this feature, is understandable because such economies have no other industries into which the surplus labour on the land can be absorbed.

It is regrettable but undoubtedly true that the British economy shares in some respects this feature of underdeveloped economies. Within both the public and the private sectors there is substantial over-manning in both industry and office work. The reason for this waste is partly historical, e.g. the economic depression of the inter-war years and its impact upon public attitudes. Yet, even in periods of crippling labour shortages such practices have continued. The reasons for this inertia are many; the nation lacks both a policy and adequate facilities for re-deploying surplus labour; re-training centres for redundant employees are in short supply; post-war housing policy has discouraged mobility of labour rather than facilitating it; the present structure of social security benefits does nothing to encourage people to change jobs, and last but not least trades unions have not been markedly co-operative over the re-employment of men trained in government training centres.

The lack of public concern over this waste of the nation's most valuable economic resource is in large measure due to successive governments' unwillingness to pursue rational long-term policies which, in the short run at least, might alienate some electoral support. As far as the employee and the trades unions are concerned, their attitude to the matter is at least comprehensible. Industry, in the present state of labour relations, has for obvious reasons been unwilling to do anything as long as Ministers of the Crown have ignored the matter and found it politically more advantageous to disburse taxpayer's money to maintain 'full' employment.

All the worst features of this depressing situation are in evidence as the economic situation deteriorates. Taxpayers' money is handed out to companies which have only the remotest prospect of making profits. Unrealistic pay increases are granted in the nationalized industries to both the labour force required and that which is surplus to requirements. The resultant losses of these basic industries are then described as the consequence of subsidies to the consumer! While the economic consequences of such policies are deplorable, even more reprehensible is the total lack of will on the part of those concerned, i.e. government, employers and the trades unions, to discuss the matter in public, much less to do anything about it. After all, trades unions do not sponsor their Parliamentary candidates for nothing.

Tempting as it is to conclude that this situation is a product of the mixed economy and the Welfare State, restrictive practices of one kind and another are much older. It was not until after the last war that a Labour Government legislated to control industrial monopoly to any extent, but the problem had attracted the attention of economists in the 1880s when Britain's economic domination of the world's markets was first eroded. The economic implications of restrictive practices are nowhere more lucidly or simply examined than in the writings of Alfred Marshall (1842–1924) who, between 1885 and 1908, occupied the Chair of Political Economy in the University of Cambridge.

Apart from his contribution to the creation of a systematic body of economic analysis and the integration into his theory of value and the workings of the market place of earlier British and European writing, what makes Marshall so interesting even to the present-day student of economics is his continuing awareness of the world within which economic forces function. The student of economics reared on a diet of post-Keynesian and Hicksian theory may well echo sympathetically the comment by Professor E. Ronald Walker in his book *From Economic Theory to Policy* that 'the resulting body of economic doctrine is inevitably more remote from practical affairs than were the writings of Adam Smith or even Alfred Marshall.' (p. 5).

In his preface to *Industry and Trade* Alfred Marshall describes how he had collected many years previously much of the information upon which the book was based. He 'set himself to obtain some insight into industrial problems by visiting representative works in each chief industry . . . to understand the resources and mode of operation of all elementary plant and to study the relations between technique and the conditions of employment for men and women. . . . I made it a practice to ask what pay was being earned by each class of operative whom I passed. Afterwards I asked to be allowed to guess in every case; if my guess was within a shilling or two a week, I passed on. If not, I asked for an explanation, and I almost always found that the reason lay in a cause, sometimes technical, sometimes relating to special conditions of the workers in question which I did not know. The result was conviction that inequalities of pay were less arbitrary than was often asserted and were more directly under the influence of broad "natural" causes.'

'But,' he continued in his preface, 'I believed that the causes were not wholly beyond human control and that they might probably be so modified as to bring about a nearer approach to equality of conditions and a better use of the products of human effort for the benefit of humanity. I developed a tendency to socialism, which was fortified later on by Mill's essay in the *Fortnightly Review* in 1879. Thus, for more than a decade, I remained under the conviction that the suggestions which are associated with the word 'socialism' were the most important subject of study, if not in the world yet at all events for me. But the writings of socialists generally repelled me almost as much as they attracted me because they seemed so far out of touch with reality . . .'

Whatever one's reaction to this glimpse of the 'inner man', it has to be conceded that throughout Alfred Marshall's voluminous writings his observation of the then current industrial scene clearly influenced his thinking on what we would now describe as 'labour economics'. Consider, for example, the following passage from his *Economics of Industry* (p. 384).

> 'In those trades which are much subject to the bracing action of foreign competition . . . a quick nemesis has followed on any quarrelsome or obstructive tendencies that have hindered in any way, direct or indirect, the full efficiency of human energies and the material invested in the trade. Any injury that a union may cause to the employers, not being capable of being passed on to the consumers, acts quickly upon the supply of capital in the trade and therefore reacts on the wages of the employed.'

Ignoring the somewhat dated prose style, can the validity of this observation even in the era of the Welfare State be contested when one surveys the developments in the London docks during the past decade?

Marshall has some highly apposite comments upon union militancy in the same text. Thus,

> 'the disturbing effects of trade union action are probably seen at their maximum in trades which have a monopoly of some special skill and are not much influenced by fear of foreign competition. It is in some of these trades that a bad use of trade union force is most likely to show itself; a use that injures employers in the first instance but in the longer run is chiefly at the expense of the general public' (p. 388).

The relevance of Marshall's conclusions is equally obvious in the following quotation:

> '. . . the belief that wages can be raised generally and permanently by checking the supply of labour . . . underestimates the effects (of such a policy) on the supply of capital . . . A considerable part of the cost will doubtless fall on employers and capitalists . . . some will fall on consumers. Ultimately, a considerable part of the burden resulting from the shrinkage of the national dividend [gross national income in modern parlance] would doubtless be thrown on other classes of the nation, and especially on the capitalists for a time, but only for a time. For a considerable diminution in the net return to investments of capital would speedily drive new supplies of it abroad' (p. 357).

Small wonder that Fords look across the Channel to W. Germany or to Spain or that there is speculation whether Chrysler may close some of its British plants. In his comment that 'in trades which have any sort of monopoly, [workers] by limiting their numbers may secure very high wages at the expense partly of their employers but chiefly at the expense of the community' (p. 395). Marshall could never have realized how accurately his words would describe the present-day situation in Fleet Street.

One need look no further than Marshall to learn what it costs the nation when dock labour in the North-east can claim up to £4,000 per annum to watch the container ships go by; or when management and labour cannot agree on a price for operating new equipment such as the automatic sorting equipment acquired by the Post Office some years ago. Thus, commenting on the need to exploit fully the available capital investment, he writes,

> 'the arts of production would progress more rapidly; the national dividend would increase; working men would be able to earn higher wages without checking the growth of capital or tempting it to migrate to countries where wages are lower, and all classes would reap the benefit of the change' (p. 353).

Marshall is not concerned with the question of whether trades unions and their activities are in themselves good or bad. His purpose in reviewing such matters is 'to enquire whether, by a judicious use of the threat of temporarily withholding the supply of labour, unions can force employers and through them the community at large, to pay higher wages' (p. 368). He is certainly not antagonistic. Of the Combination Acts he writes: 'these laws have made a crime of what was no crime' and continues 'Men who know that they are criminals by the mere object which they have in view, care little for the additional criminality involved in the means they adopt' (p. 362). And there is more to come.

> 'They knew the law was full of class injustice; destruction of life and property, when it was wrought for the purpose of enforcing what they thought justice, seemed to them to have a higher sanction than that of the law.'

It seems the apologists for the Shrewsbury pickets could well have invoked Alfred Marshall in their defence!

Nor could any trade union official fault Alfred Marshall's summary of the objectives of trades unions, i.e. 'the increase in wages, the reduction of the hours of labour, the securing of healthy, safe, and pleasant conditions of work, and defending individual workers from arbitrary and unjust treatment by their employers' (p. 363). And, to crown it all, 'the better organized a union is, the smaller is the chance that a local quarrel will mature into a strike . . .' 'The unwillingness of employers to try conclusions with (a strong union) and the prudence of the officials of such a union . . . tend to diminish the number of strikes' (p. 378). Since at the time Marshall was writing the shopfloor militant had not begun to emerge, one can only regret that currently the role of the trades unions is not quite as Marshall described it.

Even in his time, however, the unions were not without some shortcomings, although it must be conceded that there was rather more justification for any 'militancy' than there is in most cases of industrial dispute nowadays. 'Trades unions', writes Marshall, in *Industry and Trade* (p. 639), 'have in some cases systematized a practice which has prevailed in many workshops, without any formal organization. It is to censure and, in some cases, penalize anyone who appears to them to injure the collective interests of the workers by doing more than his share of the work.' But, claims Marshall, such a worker 'makes the machine diligent and the reward of its diligence goes partly to the operative and partly to the employer who has secured his services. But his comrades look askance . . . because it invites a reduction of the piecework price and because it uses up more than they regard as one man's share of the work on hand.'

The notion that the conditions of the working classes generally can be improved by such practices is, according to Marshall, erroneous. Indeed, he claims, such notions are 'the chief cause of the most bitterly anti-social policies into which the working classes have ever strayed' (p. 640). No doubt, he concedes, 'the chief immediate sufferers are as a rule particular employers; but such stinting of production is most common in industries which make goods for general consumption and, therefore, in the long run the working classes are themselves the chief sufferers from it.' Marshall's reaction to this union practice is interesting. He comments on the 'exceptional degree' to which British artisans have lent themselves to this practice and of 'refusing to manage more than one semi-automatic machine at a time', behaviour which stands out 'in strange contrast to the general nobility and generosity of their character; for that appears not to be surpassed, even if it is equalled among the corresponding classes of any other nation' (p. 641). He seeks to explain the persistence of these practices – 'stinting of production' as arising from the time when British technology was far ahead of our competitors and thus the workers had 'little to fear from external competition'. But now . . . 'there is scarcely any industrial plant in Britain which has not its equal in America or some other country and' . . . such refusals on the part of British artisans 'to get the most that is possible out of her plant tend to make her position as a leader lower than it would otherwise be.' It is doubtful, however, whether any of the workers in the engineering and motor industry facing possible redundancy would fully appreciate the logic of Marshall's observations.

No reader of these brief excerpts from Alfred Marshall's references to labour could conclude that he was hostile to organized labour. He saw the trades unions as part of the institutional framework of society and, as he so rightly observed in his *Money, Credit & Commerce* (p. 260), 'economic institutions are the products of human nature and cannot change faster than human nature changes.' And, he concluded, 'we have to act for the present and take human nature, not as it may be, but as it is.'

Marshall was concerned with the effects on the national economy, through their impact upon costs and prices, of trade union action. To the extent that trades unions prevented the most effective use of the resources available the 'national dividend', or the g.n.p. as we prefer to call it, was smaller than it would otherwise have been and, to this extent, the working classes were the losers. But he had full sympathy with the worker, as may be seen from his comment on unemployment in *Money, Credit & Commerce* at pp. 260–1:

> '. . . forced interruption to labour is a grievous evil. Those whose livelihood is secure, gain physical and mental health from happy and well-spent holidays. But want of work, with long continued anxiety, consumes a man's best strength without any return. His wife becomes thin and his children get, as it were, a nasty notch in their lives, which is perhaps never quite overcome.'

Marshall was hardly a prophet; he never sought to be such. The measure of his contribution is evident from the simple fact that, as the selection of quotations have sought to show, however much the social structure of our society may change, economic forces are the same today as they were a century ago. The only difference is that some of the population can be insulated against the impact of those forces at the expense of others in the community. Efforts to restrain the working of such economic forces, as Marshall sought to emphasize, merely lead in the longer run to a lower aggregate national dividend than would otherwise have been produced. That conclusion is as relevant to the socialist State as it is to a free enterprise society; economics as taught by Marshall does not discriminate.

And, lest any reader should feel that Marshall was concerned only marginally with the economic problems which nowadays beset the U.K. economy, let him consider the following passage from *Industry & Trade* at p. 659:

> 'If Britain is to hold her place in the world, her growing population ever more dependent on external supplies of food and materials must be provided with enlarged and improved mechanical appliances for production; and therefore ever greater net additions to her accumulated capital must be made in order that her national dividend may be as large relatively to her population . . . as before the war . . . If everyone will get as much work as possible out of his plant while in charge of it and, in those industries in which the plant is very expensive, will agree to work in shifts so as to keep the plant at work for twice as long as the normal working day, the wages will be raised automatically far above their present level . . .'

Convert the language into the post-war idiom and you have the set speech made by every Prime Minister since 1947. Perhaps Marshall was, after all, a prophet.

KEYNES – DISHONOURED BY DISCIPLES?

MALCOLM HOPPE

When John Maynard Keynes died on Easter Sunday, 1946, the Age of Keynes had scarcely begun. Thirty years on, Keynesian economics is in danger of being discredited as the Western world grapples with inflation and more people ask 'Was Keynes right?' Time deals harshly with the memories of great men, and it would be surprising if some reassessment did not reveal flaws in the image. But the impact of Keynes on our times has been so pervasive that many continue to regard him as 'the greatest economist of the twentieth century'.

In a century three-quarters gone, the Age of Keynes has existed for about half that period. In that age the free enterprise economy has suffered more and more from interventions by government. The fault should not be laid at Keynes's door alone. Other influences have been more pernicious and damaging under Keynes's influence. Governments in virtually all Western industrialized countries have come to accept as a major part of their policies management of the economy to preserve a high level of employment.

Keynes's memorial is that unemployment has not again approached the levels that persisted for almost the whole of the inter-war period. Since the last war unemployment in the United Kingdom has averaged little more than one and a half per cent of the working population. From 1920–40 it only once fell below ten per cent and exceeded twenty per cent in the early 1930s. The post-1945 unemployment level has, moreover, been generally lower than the levels experienced before 1914. It has been said that Keynes rescued capitalism and gave it humanity,

His major work, *The General Theory of Unemployment, Interest and Money*, appeared in 1936. It immediately divided economists into those who found it a persuasive answer to the problems of the Depression and those who found in it a dangerously inflationary doctrine. The impact of the 'General Theory' on official policy was not so swift. Keynes himself forecast that in ten years it would change the way the world thought about economic problems. His timescale was about right.

The General Theory challenged the accepted classical doctrine of the 'invisible hand' at work in economic affairs to ensure that economics were brought into balance at a point where full employment existed. Keynes argued that the balance was determined by many decisions to save and to invest, and there was no reason to suppose that they would automatically coincide at the level of full employment. In short, it was possible for an economy to be in balance but with a deficiency in demand for resources, which remained unused. Keynes urged that governments should step in to remove the deficiency.

The instrument of government action was to be a budgetary deficit. Until then budgets were regarded as merely a means of balancing government income and expenditure. According to Keynes, Chancellors should aim at increasing expenditure or cutting taxes in order to increase demand where unemployment warranted it. If demand was excessive, causing bottlenecks and inflation, there should be a surplus in the budget of taxes over expenditure.

In 1941 Keynes saw his principles adopted in the Kingsley Wood budget, the first in Britain specifically designed with any eye to influencing the balance of the economy rather than the government's own book-keeping. And in 1944 Keynes (now Lord Keynes) achieved another landmark in the White Paper on Employment Policy. For the next thirty years this was the guiding plan for economic policy in Britain. In the United States the Employment Act of 1946 gave qualified support for his ideas, indicating the federal government's responsibility to take positive action to reduce unemployment.

In the United States unemployment rates, even when adjustments are made for differing methods of measurement, have remained considerably higher than in this country. But, at four to five per cent, they have been much better than in pre-war days. Failure to bring them down still further may be due to continued qualified application of Keynesian economic management.

Nevertheless, in government circles throughout the Western developed world conversion to Keynesian concepts was extensive. How great was the 'revolution' and how far was Keynes responsible for it? He has never converted all economists, particularly those who from the early days believed his ideas must result in increasing inflation. It is also true that Keynes was not alone at this time in his advocacy of increased government expenditure to combat unemployment. Dennis Robertson, Hubert Henderson, A. C. Pigou, Henry Clay and other distinguished economists all favoured public works programmes. Indeed, public works expenditure did not emerge suddenly at this time. It was not unknown before 1914 as a means of reducing the effect of fluctuations in the trade cycle, and Roosevelt's New Deal made great use of it.

Yet Keynes's voice was the most persuasive. It is said his system was incomplete and did not allow for the other factors influencing unemployment. It is also claimed that he exaggerated the extent of his challenge to existing economic theory. Answers to both charges are to be found in Keynes's personality.

He was not concerned, unlike Marshall, with a need to erect a rounded system, as complete as possible in order to forestall criticism. He was concerned to treat the disease he saw before him. In the 1930s it was unemployment. His friend and colleague, Austin Robinson, declared that if Keynesian economics is now seen as a set of panaceas for the economic disease of the 1930s applied uncritically to the entirely different world of the 1960s and 1970s, Keynes himself would not be a Keynesian.[1]

The essence of Keynesianism, as Keynes indicated it would, lies in a way of looking at economic problems. Professor Robinson argues that in this sense almost all economists today are

1. Inaugural Keynes Lecture, to the British Academy, 22 April, 1971.

Keynesians. They approach the problems of the whole economy by looking at aggregates – savings, investment, production capacity – to see how far they are affecting the operation of the economy and its expansion without more inflation than is tolerable.

Since Keynes the style of economic management has changed radically. It cannot be held, however, that application (or misapplication) of his principles has kept inflation within tolerable bounds. The history of the post-war world is marked by steadily rising rates of inflation. And the course of economic management has been increasingly erratic, proceeding ever more rapidly from its expansionist to its deflationary phases.

Anti-Keynesians considered this to be the inevitable outcome of Keynesian concepts. They would argue that government stimulation of the economy leads to over-expansion of the money supply. This is followed by rising prices and costs that – certainly in Britain – lead quickly to a balance of payments crisis. Corrective action is followed by a rise in unemployment. So a further application of Keynesian expansion operates, setting in train a new cycle. Keynesian formulae provide no prescription for breaking into the cycle, but each successive round requires a greater expansion of the money supply and a higher rate of inflation to maintain the same level of employment.

One can disagree whether these consequences stem from Keynesian economics as stated by Keynes or from an unwavering adherence by neo-Keynesians to ideas that no longer fit contemporary conditions. There is good reason to believe that Keynes would have altered his views had he lived.

Friedrich von Hayek, perhaps the leading critic of Keynes, has provided support for this belief. Professor Hayek attributes much of the post-war inflation to the great influence of 'over-simplified Keynesianism'. 'Not that Keynes would have approved of this,' he has written. 'Indeed, I am fairly certain that if he had lived he would in that period have been one of the most determined fighters against inflation'[2].

2. "Personal Recollections of Keynes and the 'Keynesian Revolution'" (The Oriental Economist, January 1966; reprinted in 'A Tiger by the Tail', Institute of Economic Affairs, 1972).

Hayek recalls a meeting with Keynes only a few weeks before his death. It convinced him that Keynes would have rebelled against the interpretations placed upon his theories. Asked by Hayek whether he was not alarmed at the use of these theories by some of his disciples, Keynes replied that if they ever became harmful, he would quickly bring about a change in public opinion.

Confidence in his own powers of persuasion was a feature of the Keynes legend. He always sought action and reaction. In promulgating his ideas, he wished to encourage debate and 'the co-operation of minds'. Without the guidance and restraining hand of the master, some neo-Keynesians have plunged on unwarily.

Unemployment is a social evil. But social welfare should not be measured by the single criterion of the level of unemployment. Poverty and ill-health are at least as great evils, and attempts to maintain high (some would say excessive) levels of employment have diverted resources that could otherwise have been used to raise living standards and benefit the nation's health. (Bastardisation of Keynesianism has its place in an explanation of the relatively poorer economic performance of the United Kingdom since the war by comparison with other advanced countries.)

In applying Keynesianism to the cure of post-war unemployment, governments have been guilty of failing to analyse the nature of that unemployment. Any loss of jobs, for any reason, immediately evoked a demand for expansion. The clamour for general expansion was not ameliorated by realization that labour shortages continued in the South-East of England and the Midlands, though jobs were being lost in the North or in Scotland. Again, there was a departure from Keynesian teaching.

Failure to distinguish the various types of unemployment is a potent cause of inflation. Keynes recognized that his prescription for government-instigated attacks on deficiencies in demand was aimed at what he called 'involuntary unemployment'. This was not the unemployment of people 'between jobs'. The involuntary unemployed are not those who can find jobs by moving homes, changing industries, or undergoing further training. Such structural unemployment is outside the scope of Keynesianism to cure.

In defence of Keynes, this position was clearly acknowledged in the 1944 Employment White Paper. Its authors declared that if total expenditure was expanded in an attempt to cure unemployment 'of a type due, not to the absence of jobs but to the failure of workers to move to places and occupations where they were needed, we might create a dangerous inflation'. The warning went unheeded, and the great peril of inflation has been realized. Over-simplified Keynesianism proved too seductive for politicians needing to achieve visible results in a very short time. They were attracted by the simplicity with which Keynesian policies can be activated.

Keynes's remedies can no longer be trotted out with the same complacency. Consoling voices are fewer, though they are still heard. From trade union sources comes the plea that a £1,000 million injection of public spending will turn the tide of rising unemployment yet again. The retort that this action would vastly increase inflation and undermine future employment is met with a rejoinder that we must not be too alarmed by inflation. All will be well, we are told, as long as the British rate of inflation is no higher than those of our competitors. The unpleasant fact is that the British rate is already considerably higher than those of our competitors, causing a rapid decline in the competitiveness of British goods.

For most economists, the Keynesian revolution is over. Keynesianism is seen, not as a general all-purpose theory, but as a special tract for the 1930s. Today new theories and especially new acts of political will are required. Curiously, some critics and some supporters of Keynes find themselves on the same side in urging a new policy. Marxists, who blamed Keynes for helping to preserve capitalism, and neo-Keynesians like Mrs Joan Robinson see the way forward through more State control and ownership of industry.

The latter draw their support from *The General Theory*. It is true that in the last chapter of this book Keynes foresaw a large extension of the traditional functions of government[3]. He sug-

3. The General Theory of Unemployment, Interest and Money, ch. 24, pp.379–381.

gested that further measures of socialization would be necessary, but insisted there was no obvious case for a system of State socialism embracing most of the community's economic life. Keynes specifically approved of a wide field for the exercise of private initiative and responsibility. To him, decentralization and the play of self-interest had important advantages for society.

Authoritarian State systems, he observed, *seem* (my italics) to solve the problem of unemployment at the expense of efficiency and freedom. Today, forty years after *The General Theory* was written, this view takes on greater strength. There is more evidence to show that unemployment in authoritarian States is 'hidden' and inflation is repressed. The effect on efficiency and freedom is just as damaging.

Keynes was generally liberal in politics. Although not a party man, he helped to draw up Liberal Party policies in the 1920s. While a person's political beliefs do not remain constant for all time in the face of a changing environment, Keynes's life gives no reason to suppose that he would support today's attacks on free enterprise. He defended individualism as the best safeguard of personal liberty in that it greatly widened the field for personal choice.

In summary, then, Keynes's economic remedies cannot now be relied on to prevent large-scale unemployment. The wrong and muddled application of these remedies has brought us to a situation where unemployment and inflation rise together. Moreover, the conditions of the 1960s and 1970s have changed enormously from the conditions Keynes analysed.

Rapid changes in the relative prices of energy resulting from the actions of Arab oil producers have added a new dimension to the problems of international payments and internal prices. The growth of institutions, bolstered by the great tide of legislation, have brought rigidities into our economic system so that no single act of economic management can be effective. The fact of trade union power, and the tendency of employees to resort to 'sit-ins' if faced with changing jobs, acts to frustrate normal adjustments to changes in demand.

Continued adoption of Keynesian expansionist policies removes the factor in collective bargaining that could bring the economy into balance without inflation. For, if unions price their members out of the market, governments are expected to inflate in order to fill the 'demand gap'. But the depreciation of money wages entailed leads to a new round of wage claims.

The growth of the public sector makes it impossible to bring about a redistribution of resources by deflation within a short time. Over large areas of the public sector the working of the price mechanism is suspended. Redistribution is not determined by people's preferences.

Is Keynesianism sunk without trace? Keynes's contribution to economic thought was a willingness to look at facts as they are and not to be bound by traditional opinions. The spirit of Keynes is needed today to rescue us from the traditions foisted on us by neo-Keynesians.

MILTON FRIEDMAN: LIBERTY, DIGNITY – AND MONEY

ALAN WALTERS

Milton Friedman was born sixty-two years ago, the son of poor immigrants from Eastern Europe. His mother worked as a seamstress in a sweatshop in New Jersey. She also brought up one of the great prodigies of economics and the most effective advocate of the free enterprise that provided such opportunities in the sweat shops.

Yet Friedman's brilliant career began not in economics, but in mathematical statistics. He is still recalled as the inventor of sequential analysis, which revolutionized methods of statistical quality control. Above all, he was the author of an approach to decision-making under uncertainty where apparently irrational patterns of individual behaviour, such as simultaneously insuring and gambling, are shown to be quite consistent with rationality. Even in this highly technical work, Friedman's thrust was to show that the decision of the self-regarding individual was not socially corrupt, as many do-gooders might argue, but was sensible and social.

People who like risk could take their chances while the more cautious may insure. Even if everyone starts life with equal incomes and equal innate ability, some will increase their wealth and others will reduce it, not because of a malevolent 'system', but simply because people like to order their lives in this way. (For example, why is there such an enormous spending on football pools with the consequential 'unequal' redistribution of wealth?)

Much State intervention and our so-called 'progressive tax system' is rationalized on the grounds that it redistributed wealth from the rich to the poor. But this is mere hypocrisy, albeit sincere hypocrisy. The great reforms of the liberal administrations in the United States were usually methods of redistributing income and wealth from the poor to the rich. As Friedman correctly predicted, in the United States' poverty programme much more was spent on the salaries of high-paid poverty fighters than on the poor. The expenditure is, however, massive. Indeed, Friedman once calculated that if the poor were actually paid the amount which the government had spent on poverty programmes then they would be among the better-off! The minimum wage legislation creates a larger amount of unemployment among the low-paid workers and protects the jobs of the better-off employees; by denying them jobs it injures the black teenagers particularly severely and promotes racial and other forms of discrimination.

The Social Security programme, for example, is a method of transferring income from the young to the old, whether rich or poor, and since the rich live longer and the poor start work and so begin paying earlier, it is very likely that it is simply a transfer from the poor to the better-off. The farm support programme simply pays rich farmers not to plant a crop. The urban renewal programme, a veritable triumph of urban planning, ensures that the homes of thousands of the poor are destroyed and replaced by a smaller number of superior homes for the well to do; the poor are left to crowd into the small supply of inferior accommodation as yet untouched by the social engineer's and planner's bulldozer. And so the story is broadly the same with all major State programmes.

In all these indictments Friedman has an underlying belief in the principle of individual liberty, dignity and responsibility. The sapping of self-respect and the promotion of the unsavoury artful dodgers and spongers and the erosion of a sense of responsibility are characteristics which have probably emerged more obviously in Britain than in the United States. It is not the poor who benefit but the ones who know how to pull the right strings – and they are unlikely to be the poor! Hence the difficulty with the take-up of the family income supplement and supplementary benefits. Indeed it is remarkable to observe the extent to which individual self respect and dignity have survived the assaults of the Welfare State. (Am I alone in wondering at the great incentive to work shown by low paid employees in the U.K.? The unemployment welfare benefits plus a little-on-the-side are far more attractive than work.)

Of course, the welfare legislators and the many people who support and vote for such policies are not wicked men bent on the destruction of the family and self respect. On the contrary, they are . . . 'well meaning reformers (who) go to Washington to do good and end up doing harm'. It is typical of Friedman's generous spirit that he is always prepared to see the best motives behind the worst actions.

Noble efforts to redistribute income through graduated taxes are common to all parties. The income tax, even more in Britain than in the United States, is a combination of nominally steeply-escalating rates (up to a marginal rate of 98 per cent and even more in real terms). But a tissue of loopholes and evasions and gentlemen's agreements have the effect of avoiding the complete destruction of incentive and thrift. Resources are wastefully invested in producing tax shelters and tax havens, and in arranging one's affairs to avoid the high rates of tax. Little is raised at the high rates. Friedman, an old employee of the Treasury Department, showed that one would get the same revenue from a flat rate tax of 16 per cent as the Federal Government now obtains from its graduated tax rates from 14 to 70 per cent. We pay dearly for our pretence at what is oddly called our 'progressive system of taxation'. More important in Britain it is likely that such high rates tempt many people to evade tax and make the law a mockery. The attempt to make the rich poor does not make the poor rich; on the contrary, it makes them even poorer.

But what of Friedman's solution to the presence of poverty? It is important first to ensure that people are not kept poor by the State (e.g. by minimum wage legislation) or by any other group, (such as trades union restrictions on entry to a trade). The residual poor, who have been given the opportunity but who cannot adequately help themselves, would qualify for State help. The best form of assistance would be a negative income tax – money rather than food coupons, free milk, free rides on public transport, subsidised rents, and the various other hand-outs in kind of the Welfare State. The negative income tax would avoid the massive army of snoopers enquiring into the most intimate details of personal affairs and it would involve a smaller loss of dignity and self respect than any of the other welfare systems. But Friedman has been insistent that the negative income tax involves a great number of difficulties, mainly connected with the effect on incentive. It remains alas only the best of regrettable necessities.

To the world at large, Friedman is known primarily as the apostle of monetarism – in the Guardian's phrase he is a 'self-confessed monetarist'. To be guilty of the crime of monetarism one must believe that 'money matters' and matters a lot. This seemingly commonsense proposition is what all the fuss is about. But in its context it is enormously important. Until sometime in the 1960s orthodox economists, bankers and chancellors and men of affairs accepted the view that the money supply was of little importance in determining either the level of activity or the rate of inflation. In order to steer or indeed in order to fine-tune the economy, the government must control spending, and particularly the purchase of investment goods, directly and it must expand or contract public expenditure to ensure the right level of money demand and the politically determined 'acceptable' percentage of unemployment. The developments of the Keynesian model provided a blanket rationalisation for nationalisation 'to secure the commanding heights of the economy' and for regulating the free market in the interests of securing a stable economy.

In an astonishing series of incisive studies Friedman showed that this conventional wisdom was a travesty of the facts. Money *did* matter, and it mattered a lot. An increase in government spending, if covered by an increase in tax revenue or by real saving on the part of the public, would have very different effects from those which would occur if the expenditure were financed by 'printing money'. Inflation is the scourge of the modern world because governments have financed their spending by increasing very rapidly the supply of money. Friedman has eloquently argued the simple age-old proposition that a glut of any commodity will cause a fall in its value. So the vast increase in the supply of money has seen the value of the currency fall and the inflation gather pace. (It may seem odd to non-economists that any professional economist should deny this obvious commonsense idea which accords so convincingly with everyday experience. But the sophists continue to cast obloquy on such simple propositions and still allege that the money supply is not important.)

Although the money supply is the dominant cause of the economic environment, its effects appear only after long and variable lags. Governments therefore cannot do any good and will, in fact, do much harm by trying to fine-tune the economy by varying the monetary conditions. The best that the authorities can do is to keep monetary conditions steady – to increase the money supply by four or five per cent per year. This will create a stable environment within which the free enterprise system can work, where the businessman will know that he will not be caught next year in a monetary squeeze (as in 1974) or have his contracts and calculations shattered by inflation (as in the occupational pension funds in the 1970s).

The present and most potent threats to the system of freedom come from inflation and the attempts by government to control it through bureaucratic regulation of prices and incomes. Such prices–incomes policies merely distort inflation; they do not stop it, they make it worse. More important they deny a fundamental human freedom – the right of anyone freely to contract, to sell and buy what he wishes at any terms he may properly settle. The economic absurdities of such a system of controls – the shortages, the queues, political favouritism, bribery, blackmarketeering, etc. – are well known. More insidious, however, is the erosion of law. The legal system and the courts are used for purposes for which they were never intended and for which they are ill-suited. Such is the welter of government control that the courts are being by-passed by new administrative courts (such as Rent Tribunals, Land Commissions, planning enquiries, Pay Boards, etc.). Characteristically, government is intervening in every facet of life and neglecting those tasks which government only can do, such as the preservation of law and order and a stable monetary environment. We get the worst of both worlds.

Friedman argued that the government's role should be to provide a framework of law applicable to all; there should be no special law for the benefit of this region, that profession, or the other industry. Law should be universal and blind to special interest. The law should not accord special rights to trades unions or to favourite communes of producers, either capitalist or co-ops, or to Clay Cross councillors to enable one group to secure a special advantage over other persons or groups. The law should provide a framework of impersonal rules applicable to all alike.

The law should not try to do what it cannot. No legal arrangements can banish poverty, selfishness, sin and suffering; nor can legislation create a heaven on earth. The law can, however, provide a framework in which each of us can strive to achieve his own ambitions while not harming and even benefiting his fellow man.

It is not easy to define exactly the boundaries of the framework of law which will best promote man's great diversity and astonishing potential. But all men who value liberty must be sure that the encroachment of the State has gone much too far. Government has increasingly taken over our lives, regulating in minute detail what we can do, taking away the fruits of our labours and either wasting it or redistributing it according to some principle of the political pay-off. At the same time, Government has made an appalling job of managing our money and maintaining law and order.

With his razor sharp intelligence and diligent and painstaking scholarship, Friedman has exposed the enormous gap between the State's high pretensions and its poor performance. With great moral courage he has swum against the mainstream of *dirigiste* economics and indeed has been largely responsible for reversing it. He believes that man will eventually learn by reason and experience that freedom under the law is the best of all possible worlds. His optimism is a triumph of his humanity, spirit, and great charity.

LUDWIG VON MISES: ANTI ANTI-CAPITALIST

MICHAEL JEFFERSON

Ludwig von Mises was one of that small band of Austrian economists who devoted their lives not merely to expounding and developing economic theory, but to defending and explaining that social order which they believed most conducive to individual freedom.

Born in 1881, he was blessed with longevity and survived – some might say in more than one sense – a two-volume festschrift on the occasion of his ninetieth birthday by a couple of years. His published work began in 1902, with an historical study of Galician peasants, and ended in 1969 with a short work on the Austrian, Neo-Classical school of economics. The intervening years were marked by a continual flow of first-rate books falling into two main groups: studies in money, inflation and the trade cycle largely produced in the inter-war period; and critiques of socialism, bureaucracy and the anti-capitalistic mentality. The latter group had their beginnings in the early 1920s, but blossomed out following von Mises' emigration to the United States in 1940. They are a goldmine for all those who are concerned at the quality of modern political debate and the increasing incursions on individual freedom.

By common consent the greatest work of von Mises is *Human Action*, published in Britain in 1949 but having its origins in a book published in German (in Switzerland) in 1940. In keeping with his intention of placing economics within a broader framework of human action, of the whole range of choices a human being can make, von Mises covers an enormous canvas with confidence and insight. He discusses philosophical matters at one moment and pricing policies or interest rates at another. And not surprisingly, if you know your man, socialism comes under heavy fire.

The socialist creed, he claims, rests upon three dogmas:

(i) Society is an omnipotent and omniscient being, free from human frailty and weakness.

(ii) The coming of socialism is inevitable.

(iii) As history is a continuous progress from less perfect conditions, the coming of socialism is desirable.

As to the first, however, the essential feature is that one will alone acts, and it is immaterial whose will it is. It may be that of a Führer or a Board of Führers, even one apparently appointed by the vote of the people. The result is that the employment of all factors of production is directed by one agency only. One will alone chooses, decides, directs, acts, gives orders; the rest obey. Organization and planned order are substituted for the 'anarchy' of the market economy and individual initiative.

The will is, nevertheless, a human being and not an abstract notion or mythical collective entity entitled Society, State or Government. It is not omniscient or infallible, however technically competent or administratively skilled. Priorities must be decided upon, projects accepted or rejected, an infinite variety of expressed or latent individual wants assessed. But even if there were agreement as to ultimate ends, hardly a likely circumstance, there is a straightforward and insuperable problem: economic calculation is impossible under socialism. The market economy may often operate imperfectly, but at least regard is paid to costs and returns of a strictly economic nature. Von Mises remarks:

> 'What is called a planned economy is no economy at all. It is just a system of groping about in the dark. There is no question of a rational choice of means for the best possible attainment

of the ultimate ends sought. What is called conscious planning is precisely the elimination of conscious purposive action.'

Von Mises places great faith in the power of human reasoning, and one reason for his individualist beliefs is that individuals have the power to think while 'the State' or 'Society' does not. Elsewhere in *Human Action* he remarks that if somebody were, at any cost, eager to distil a grain of truth out of Marxian teachings, he could say that emotions influence a man's reasoning very much.

The weakness of von Mises' position lies here, and he recognised it. He could not extricate himself from the dilemma he posed: 'the illusion of the old liberals.' The social philosophy of the Enlightenment, he records, failed to see the dangers that the prevalence of unsound ideas could engender. The classical economists and the Utilitarians, much more sensitive to the plight of the poor than is often suggested, nevertheless tended to assume that what is reasonable will carry on merely on account of its reasonableness. They overlooked the fact that public opinion could favour spurious ideologies whose realization would harm welfare and well-being and disintegrate social cooperation. (Von Mises is here a little unfair to some mid-nineteenth century writers). Conservative thinkers suffered no such illusions, but laboured under other delusions about the virtues of paternalistic governments and rigid economic institutions.

Von Mises then moves on to ground which he was to traverse many times in other, shorter works. He held firm to the belief that capitalism had given the world what it needed, a higher standard of living for a steadily increasing number of people. But the liberals who had pioneered and supported capitalism failed to appreciate sufficiently that a social system, however beneficial, cannot work if it is not supported by public opinion:

'They did not anticipate the success of the anticapitalistic propaganda. After having nullified the fable of the divine missions of anointed kings, the liberals fell prey to no less illusory doctrines, to the irresistible power of reason, to the infallibility of the *volonté générale* and to the divine inspiration of majorities.'

Again von Mises oversimplifies, but makes valid points. On the whole, liberals did believe the progress achieved under capitalism was self-evident, that its dark spots would be removed under the influence of general progress and prosperity, and that hostility would pass away on recognition of the facts. Some liberals still do, but von Mises was not among them.

It was precisely the claim that capitalism provided for a rapidly increasing population a steadily improving standard of living which many – von Mises claimed it was 'the immense majority' – did contest. To many socialist authors, and especially in the teachings of Marx, the essential point was that capitalism results in the exploitation and impoverishment of the working class. For von Mises the more impressive facts were that even in the poorer capitalist countries wealth had increased to prolong the average length of life, and the bringing up of more children would have been impossible if the means of sustenance had not been increased.

The main themes highlighted here from *Human Action*

—the internal contradictions of socialism

—the historical inadequacies of the anti-capitalistic position

and—the confusion of thought in the anti-capitalistic mentality

are brilliantly handled in three other works. In *Bureaucracy*, first published in 1944, he distinguishes profit management from bureaucratic management, bureaucratic management of private enterprises from bureaucratic management of publicly-owned enterprises, while cutting with surgical precision through the layers of socialism's contradictions. In *Theory and History*, first published in the United States in 1957, he sheds light on an enormous range of historical and other issues of present-day relevance. While in *The Anti-Capitalistic Mentality*, first published in 1956, von Mises analyses the bias and resentment of the anti-capitalistic intellectual and others, the rampant socialism and bigotry of literary and acting circles.

Von Mises defined bureaucratic management as 'the management of affairs which cannot be checked by economic calculation', in which the bureaucrat performs what the rules and regulations fixed by the authority of a superior body order him to do. Personal discretion to act according to one's own best conviction is severely limited and discouraged.

One of the interesting features of von Mises' study of bureaucracy was his handling of the bureaucratic management of private enterprises:

> 'No private enterprise,' he wrote, 'will ever fall prey to bureaucratic methods of management if it is operated with the sole aim of making profit.'

The problem is that 'ours is an age of a general attack on the profit motive', and governments frequently take steps which result in the enterprise losing its interest in increasing profits and lowering costs.

Perhaps even more fundamental, von Mises rightly saw progress of any kind as at variance with old and established ideas. Only a few people have the capacity to foresee developments and plan new things, and under capitalism the innovator is given greater encouragement than under alternative systems. In contrast, as von Mises put it:

> 'Under a bureaucratic system it is necessary to convince those at the top, as a rule old men accustomed to do things in prescribed ways, and no longer open to new ideas. No progress and no reforms can be expected in a state of affairs where the first step is to obtain the consent of the old men. The pioneers of new methods are considered rebels and are treated as such.'

Again, von Mises oversimplifies while pointing to the fundamental truths. After all, the hold of old men can work at least as much to the disadvantage of small organisations as of those which might be suspected of being large and bureaucratic. One reason is suggested by another of von Mises' remarks, in a different context:

> 'The fading of the critical sense is a serious menace to the preservation of our civilization. It makes it easy for quacks to fool the people.'

The bureaucratic management of private enterprises is frequently conducted by those with, in many respects, a highly developed critical sense. The danger is that occasional non-profit orientated tasks become routine, *ad hoc* approaches from outside organisations and agencies become increasingly acceptable and time-consuming and, in particular, government inquiry and meddling paralyzes initiative and breeds bureaucratism.

Another characteristic of our times noted by von Mises was that the better educated strata of our society are often more gullible than the less educated:

> 'The most enthusiastic supporters of Marxism, Nazism, and Fascism were the intellectuals, not the boors. The intellectuals were never keen enough to see the manifest contradictions of their creeds.'

Perhaps one of the more extraordinary characteristics of von Mises was that, while he noted these depressing features of modern society, he remained an almost incurable optimist. Take, for instance, the final words of *Theory and History*:

> 'Up to now in the West none of the apostles of stabilization and petrification has succeeded in wiping out the individual's innate disposition to think and to apply to all the problems the yardstick of reason. This alone, and no more, history and philosophy can assert in dealing with doctrines that claim to know exactly what the future has in store for mankind.'

How many people, in Britain in 1975, feel so confident? Yet von Mises himself gives us sufficient reason for deep concern. Writing about "Literature Under Capitalism" in *The Anti-Capitalistic Mentality*, he states:

> 'The essential charge brought by the progressives against capitalism is that the recurrence of crisis and depressions and mass unemployment are its inherent features.'

No thoughtful person could reasonably blame Britain's present state upon capitalism, we have had too much and too muddled government intervention for any but the ignorant or the sinister to truly believe that. But the thoughtful person must ask himself how the family on £25 per week all-in can survive; how the younger middle-classes, saddled with massive mortgages and other expenses, can keep it all up; how the market economy itself (what is left of it) can have a future when people can no longer afford to have a stake in the interests which support its creed and practices; and how socialism can fail to be unattractive to the ranks of the unemployed, to whom it is claimed their plight is due to capitalism. Under attack from every side, is the market system worth fighting for?

If confined to material self-interest, a positive answer is not immediately obvious despite the market-economy's overall efficiency. The alternative answer should principally come from a desire to retain intellectual integrity, which in turn is fortified by reactions to the bigotry and sometimes – one suspects – lack of intellectual integrity of others.

For instance, why was it necessary for von Mises, like others before him and since, to point out that independent thinkers who fundamentally question the interventionist dogmas of our day 'are virtually outlawed, and their ideas cannot reach the reading public'?

> 'The tremendous machine of "progressive" propaganda and indoctrination has well succeeded in enforcing its taboos. The intolerant orthodoxy of the self-styled "unorthodox" schools dominates the scene.'

Not merely the mass media but also, as von Mises well knew, the authors of 'socialist ("social") novels and plays':

> 'They describe unsatisfactory conditions which, as they insinuate, are the inevitable consequence of capitalism. They depict the poverty and destitution, the ignorance, dirt and disease of the exploited classes. In their eyes everything that is bad and ridiculous is bourgeois, and everything that is good and sublime is proletarian.'

How, one must ask, could anything be so one-sided and simple? How could apparently intelligent and well-educated people believe such half-baked analyses and unintelligent conclusions? Ludwig von Mises would have regarded these characteristics as a necessary pre-condition for socialist belief. For, as he put it in the closing words of *Bureaucracy*:

> 'The champions of socialism call themselves progressives, but they recommend a system which is characterized by rigid observance of routine and by a resistance to every kind of improvement. They call themselves liberals, but they are intent upon abolishing liberty. They call themselves democrats, but they yearn for dictatorship. They call themselves revolutionaries, but they want to make the government omnipotent. They promise the blessings of the Garden of Eden, but they plan to transform the world into a gigantic post office. Every man but one a subordinate clerk in a bureau, what an alluring utopia! What a noble cause to fight for!'

POPPER: THREATS TO THE OPEN SOCIETY

WILFRID SENDALL

When I was a schoolboy, I wrote in my notebook of useful quotations a paradox from Anatole France's novel, *The Revolt of the Angels*: 'The vice most fatal to a statesman is virtue: it leads to murder.' It has proved by far the most versatile epigram I ever stuffed into my journalist's ragbag of a memory. I would have recommended it to Sir Karl Popper as the text of his great work: *The Open Society and its Enemies*.

For Sir Karl's purpose is to demonstrate the proposition that, in human affairs, the ideal is the greatest enemy of the good. In his words: 'The attempt to make heaven on earth invarably produces hell.' He traces with brilliant perception the way in which virtuous men, from Plato, through Hegel, to Karl Marx, have been led by their virtue to advocate the murder of both ideas and of people.

Sir Karl shows that it is the aim of the idealist to arrest change once his ideal society has been established, whether it be Plato's Republic, Hegel's nation-state or Marx's classless society. To arrest change, it is necessary to destroy freedom. If in doing so it becomes necessary to kill people, then so be it. Marx, in fact, emerges as the more humane. Once the dictatorship of the proletariat had been reached, he did not imagine that any killing would be needed. Lenin and his successors have proved how wrong that was.

The particular question to which I am asked to devote this essay is the relevance of this thesis to the situation today. How does it relate, if at all, to our current political controversies? My answer is to contend that the idealist element in the British Labour Party has acquired such strength that it may lead to the murder of the idea which the vast majority of the party's supporters cherish most – the system of parliamentary democracy.

In 1949 one of Clement Attlee's closest personal adherents said to me: 'It is no part of my belief that democracy is a one-way street.' I suspect he was quoting his master. I contrast that remark with the statement in *Labour's Programme 1973* that the goal is 'to bring about a fundamental and *irreversible* shift in the balance of power and wealth . . .' I cannot reconcile the two statements. I shy at the use of the word 'irreversible'.

Liberals in the Labour Party – and there are still plenty of them – would point to the concluding words of the sentence: '. . . in favour of working people and their families'. They would ask: 'Who would want to reverse that?' But to assert that it would be undesirable to reverse any act of government is not the same thing as to say that it should be irreversible.

It is true, also, that the expression 'working people' is meaningless, as virtually everybody in our community, headed by the Duke of Edinburgh, would claim to be a working person. Unhappily, we know that it was used by its authors in the Marxist sense of the 'working class'. If we altered the sentence to read 'in favour of university graduates and their families', or 'members of the Church of England and their families', we should recognise the sinister implication.

As Sir Karl Popper argues, the essential characteristic of a democracy is the power of the ruled to dismiss the rulers without violence. Indeed, it emerges from his argument that the right to get rid of the rulers is more important than the right to choose them. To have any meaning, this must imply the right to reverse any of their actions. In Britain, this is embodied in the doctrine that no Parliament can bind its successors.

To be fair to the Labour Party, I do not think many of them are aware that they are attacking so vital a principle. I have enough experience of the drafting of political manifestos to know how slipshod the wording usually is. But I also know that words are often chosen *because* they are slipshod, because thus they afford a basis for superficial agreement between groups whose motives are sharply opposed. Later one group or another will attach to the words selected a meaning repulsive to the others who complacently agreed to them.

I suspect that this is what happened with regard to Labour's programme, and that those who know precisely what they mean by irreversible are the Marxists. This brings one immediately to consideration of what methods might be used to prevent the reversal of current policies by a successor government. We have been warned very clearly of the possibilities. We have recent experience of successful industrial action to frustrate the policies of a Government in office with a Parliamentary majority, and of the ambiguous reaction even of so-called moderates in the Labour Party to this development. There can be no room for doubt that the weapon in mind to stop reversal of actions of the present government is the political strike.

Sir Karl Popper warns of the risks to democracy in resort to this action. Like that of some Labour politicians, however, his attitude is somewhat ambiguous. It must be remembered that he was writing during the war and most strongly under the influence of events in Germany immediately prior to it. He is conscious of the potentiality of the strike weapon *as a defence* of democracy, citing the case of the Kapp putsch against the Weimar Republic in 1920, which was frustrated by a general strike of the workers of Berlin. Nevertheless his condemnation of the political strike as an *offensive* weapon is unequivocal.

The very fact that his trumpet sounds an uncertain note on this issue should emphasise the danger for the genuinely democratic majority of Labour supporters. Strikes to prevent the reversal or modification of acts of the present government are going to be represented as *defensive* of democracy. Let it be clearly proclaimed, here and now, that a strike to frustrate the democratic right of any elected government to reverse the acts of its predecessor is a deadly blow at the heart of democracy. It would be a precedent for future rulers to resist by violence their dismissal by the ruled. Sir Karl Popper's statement that anti-democratic action by the workers 'must provide their own enemies, and those of democracy, with an opportunity' should stand without any qualification.

Assuredly Labour politicians would happily accept a general description of their policies as interventionist, embraced by what Sir Karl Popper calls 'social engineering'. But the description applies equally well to the policies of the Conservative Party, indeed to the policies of any serious political party in any developed industrial society. Unqualified 'laissez faire' nowadays is dead.

This fact, however, makes Sir Karl's analysis of his own expression, breaking it down into different categories of social engineering, perhaps the most obviously relevant and topical of his contributions.

As virtually the whole of modern politics is a matter of social engineering, it is important to know what we are talking about. Sir Karl Popper draws a careful distinction between 'Utopian engineering' and 'piecemeal engineering', utterly condemning the first but extending qualified approval to the second. His approval is qualified by a sub-division into 'institutional engineering', which he advocates, and 'personal or direct engineering', about which he has doubts.

Utopian engineering is radical and revolutionary. It involves the destruction of existing society, what Plato calls 'making the canvas clean', and then proceeding to the construction of a new, ideal society as a whole. It is wholly authoritarian in conception and Sir Karl abominates it as about the worst enemy of his Open Society, for, to achieve it, it becomes imperative to 'purify, purge, expel, banish and kill'. (How directly Anatole France got to the point!)

As Sir Karl reminds us, Marx also condemned it, as he condemns all social engineering, for Marx believed that the collapse of capitalism and the arrival of the classless society was an historic inevitability, so that political action was largely irrelevant. However, as a matter of fact, Lenin attempted a vast essay in Utopian engineering, which quickly collapsed, driving him back on piecemeal engineering in the New Economic Policy, for which Marxism offered him no guidance whatsoever.

The most notorious attempt at Utopian social engineering was that of Hitler. To reach the perfect Hegelian nation-state, he put in hand the atrocious 'final solution of the Jewish problem'. The contemporary example of the method is apartheid.

For the purposes of contemporary British politics, the pure form of Utopian engineering is irrelevant. What is relevant is a kind of piecemeal engineering with a Utopian purpose (my personal gloss on the Popper analysis). This involves, not making the canvas clean, but just rubbing a bit of it clean and filling in the space a section of the Utopian picture, with the overall purpose that, eventually, all the bits of the jig-saw will fit together to form a complete Utopia.

There is a topical instance of this method in the Labour Party's plan for uniform comprehensive education. Its Utopian aim is to bring about an equalitarian society. The first step is to rub out all the non-comprehensive or independent schools. The viciousness of this policy is that it is, for all intents and purposes, irreversible. Once uniformity has been created, it becomes practically impossible, or at least very difficult, to re-create diversity.

For our purposes, however, the two sub-divisions of piecemeal engineering are the most significant. Piecemeal engineering means tackling a particular and identifiable social evil by relatively limited measures, without worrying about any ultimate vision of perfection.

The institutional method proceeds by the creation of institutions and laws applicable to the problem, such as social insurance, public health and factory legislation. Usually these operate indirectly, by influencing the conduct of individuals in the desired direction. The advantage of the method is that it is infinitely adjustable in the light of practical experience and that it establishes a consistent framework within which individuals can make their personal judgments and decisions.

The direct or personal method involves empowering Ministers or servants of the State directly to require individuals to perform certain actions or to desist from them. It is open to serious objections in that it is unpredictable, often inconsistent, even capricious, and liable to lead to bureaucratic tyranny. Both methods are in constant use by all governments in this country.

Conservative political doctrine emphatically favours the institutional method, though in practice Conservative governments have too easily slipped into the use of the direct method. In the Labour Party a predilection for the second method is growing rapidly, being endorsed by doctrine as well as employed in practice.

Sir Karl Popper writes:

> 'There can be no doubt, from the point of view of democratic control, which of these methods is preferable.
>
> The obvious policy for all democratic intervention is to make use of the first method wherever it is possible, and to restrict the use of the second method to cases for which the first method is inadequate.'

Labour's Programme 1973 proclaims total impatience and dissatisfaction with the institutional method of social engineering.

> 'The experience of Labour Governments has made it increasingly evident that even the most comprehensive measures of social and fiscal reform can only succeed in masking the unacceptable and unpleasant face of a capitalist economy, and cannot achieve any fundamental change in the power relationships which dominate our society.'

The outcome of this pronouncement was the Industry Bill, which constitutes the largest extension of the method of direct or personal social engineering in British experience. Sir Karl's comment is apt. 'Governments live from hand to mouth, and discretionary powers belong to this style of living – *apart from the fact that rulers are inclined to love these powers for their own sake.*'

The obsession of the Labour Party with the transfer of economic power – 'Economic power must be transferred from a small elite to the mass of the people' – derives from a false equation that wealth equals power. This fallacy is Marxist in origin and accounts for Marx's contempt for political democracy.

In *The Open Society* this fallacy is exposed. Sir Karl Popper concludes that economic power is entirely dependent on political and physical power and, though money can buy power, this is only possible to a strictly limited extent. He refers to instances cited by Bertrand Russell illustrating the dependence, even the helplessness of wealth, and writes:

> 'The dogma that economic power is the root of all evil must be discarded. Its place must be taken by an understanding of the dangers of *any* form of uncontrolled power . . . We must realise that control of physical power and of physical exploitation is the central political problem.'

If this is true, the Labour Party in its State acquisition programme is chasing a red herring. In this country at present physical power is firmly under democratic political control. Our central political problem is to keep it so. The mere transfer of industrial assets from private to State ownership does not help in the slightest. It could do harm. But the truth is that, in spite of the verbiage in its propaganda, the Labour Party does not really appeal to the fear of wealth, for few people in Britain really fear it. What they appeal to is the *envy* of wealth, which is a very different matter.

Sir Karl Popper does not examine the historical origin of the assertion that wealth and power are identical. Indeed, he appears suspicious of any study of historical origins lest it leads to the deadly sin of 'historicism', by which he means the claim to deduce from history some immutable law or pattern which determines the future. This is a pity, because such an investigation into the relationship of wealth and power might have led him to develop consideration of another relationship, that between a free enterprise economy and free political institutions.

For the greater part of man's existence, wealth and power have been in fact identical. When all wealth was derived from the cultivation of land, there was only one way in which it could be accumulated, by physical possession of the land itself and by the enslavement of human creatures to cultivate it. In such circumstances – and they prevailed for a very long time – physical power was wealth. Wealth and power could not be separated. In such circumstances, moreover, political freedom was an impossible conception. It simply could not exist, though there could be greater or lesser degrees of tyranny.

Political freedom only starts to appear with the separation of wealth and power, when sources of wealth arose which did not need physical power, in short with the development of commerce. Sir Karl Popper picks up this theme only briefly with reference to Athens, the first community to move into an Open Society.

He shows how Athenian democracy, the great society which Pericles extolled in the famous funeral oration, depended on the Long Walls linking the fortress of the Acropolis with the harbours of the Piraeus and Phalerum. 'It became clear to (the oligarchs) that the trade of Athens, its monetary commercialism, its naval policy and its democratic tendencies were parts of one single movement, and it was impossible to defeat democracy without going to the roots of the evil and destroying both the naval policy and the empire'.

To my mind there could be no clearer exposition of the relationship between free political institutions and a free enterprise commerce, from which wealth could be derived without power. True, it was necessary to *buy* physical power in the form of a navy to protect the commerce. True, the power thus bought was later used to destroy the freedom of other cities, the fatal error which poisoned the great society. But neither of these facts invalidates the argument that the first requirement of democracy is a source of wealth that is separate from power.

The first flickerings of freedom in Western Europe are found in the Italian cities, with their rich trade and monetary commercialism, in the Flemish cities with their cloth-making industry and trade, in the Netherlands, and in England with the development of the wool trade and the seaborne commerce of the city of London.

If the historic relationship I have briefly traced has any validity, it makes nonsense of Tawney's description of the free enterprise system, which the Labour Party gleefully quotes, as 'the arbitrary exercise of economic power'. For it demonstrates that the free enterprise system produces its own corrective, by the stimulation of free political institutions capable of bringing the economy under the discipline of democratic political power. It would be folly indeed now to divert that political power towards the destruction of the very system which gave it birth.

I am aware that if I ventured to assert the relationship of the free enterprise economy with free political institutions as an immutable law, I might be guilty of what Sir Karl Popper would reckon the dangerous error of historicism. Nevertheless, I am inclined to believe that a case could be developed for an indissoluble relationship between the two which would be very difficult to refute. It might also be possible to go a step further to argue that free political institutions could not possibly survive the destruction of a free enterprise economy. But I will stop at saying that I cannot think of any historical instance in which they have done so.

To go further would be to pose as a prophet, and Sir Karl tells us that 'instead of posing as prophets we must become the makers of our fate'.

Instead of making our fate, at present we are doing little more than frivolously and haphazardly meddling with it. The fault of our social engineering is that too often we are seeking remedies for the wrong ailment. In other words, the Labour Party and their trade union allies, who happen to have the power at this moment, are busy fighting the battle which has already been effectively won.

Sir Karl Popper encourages us to believe that we can interpret history to aid in the fight for the Open Society. But the social engineers are prone simply to scrap through history to pick out the bits which seem to justify what they have already decided to do. There is little attempt at what I would call the 'clinical' study of history, in the spirit in which a physician analyses the symptoms of past cases to guide his diagnosis of new ones.

But we cannot stop meddling. We cannot passively submit to the action and influence of natural forces. Besides, why should we? In spite of all the blundering, as H. A. L. Fisher has said: 'The fact of progress is written plain and large on the pages of history'. Man has not done too bad a job so far as a maker of his fate.

'But', Fisher adds (with the endorsement of Popper), 'progress is not a law of nature. The ground won by one generation may be lost by the next'.

If we heed that warning, if we intend to avoid being a generation of losers, we should beware of discarding arrogantly and hastily any of the tools which hitherto have manifestly helped humanity to do the job.

F. A. HAYEK: NEXT CONSTRUCTION FOR THE GIANT

PEREGRINE WORSTHORNE

The one freedom – apart from that of choosing one's own government – which most British people still take seriously is the freedom to say and write what one wants to say and write: freedom of expression. Any attempt by the State to infringe it immediately runs into a storm of remonstrance. The media can be relied upon to thunder mightily in its defence, since this particular freedom still enjoys an almost sacred place in the pantheon of human rights, arousing near religious faith and fervour. In this respect, at any rate, it can truly be said that freedom is still a living principle – one for which many people would be prepared to die.

Fine! We must be grateful for small mercies, and thank God that there is at least one area of human behaviour where freedom is felt to be vitally valuable, not to say essential. But why only in this area? At a time when the State can get away with interfering and controlling pretty well every other area, why has this particular one been singled out as so specially worth defending?

The routine answer is that freedom of expression is overridingly important, the father and mother of all other freedoms, the only one that really matters. I find this proposition very difficult to accept, except in circumstances which certainly do not apply at the present time. If one could assume that freedom of expression would always be used to protect other freedoms, that those who made use of the right to write what they want would use it to help defend the rights of others to do what they want, then there might be some truth in the view that this was the one freedom on which the rest depended.

Historically this used to be the case, or sufficiently so to help explain how this assumption grew up. British history contains a glorious catalogue of examples of how the right to speak and write freely was used to extend the frontiers of freedom generally. Radical writers and speakers used their freedom of expression to champion the libertarian cause as a whole, very often thereby running into fierce State opposition, even suppression. This was very much the pattern of the eighteenth and nineteenth centuries when the State certainly had an interest in suppressing or limiting freedom of expression, since it tended to be used then to champion all sorts of causes that had to do with the expansion of individual rights and the diminution of State authority.

But that is scarcely the case today. The most influential writers and speakers today, those who make most use of the freedom of expression, tend on balance to be in favour of State power and to argue for its extension rather than its limitation. Few surely would deny that in the last half-century or so the impact of the written and spoken word had been largely in the direction of aggrandising the State, at the expense of individual freedom. Far from the cherished freedom of expression acting as the great protector of all freedoms, it has tended, more often than not, to be used by those who have very different ends in view, who have used their freedom to write and say what they feel and think to argue the case for preventing their fellow citizens from *doing* much that they want to do.

This is not to imply that freedom of expression is not a vastly-important principle. Manifestly it is, for reasons so familiar as not to need emphasizing here. What does need pointing out, however, is that it is not necessarily the father and mother of all other freedoms; nor in all circumstances the one that deserves most respect and protection. Indeed, the belief that all freedoms are safe if this one freedom is safe can prove – indeed is proving – highly dangerous, since those who make use of the freedom of expression, like those who make use of every other freedom, can by no stretch of the imagination any longer be assumed to be concerned with the freedom of all.

For the truth is that those who for the most part make use of the freedom of expression, who have the skill and the inclination to do so, can only be relied upon to understand freedom in so far as it is relevant and essential to their own special activity, which has to do with the dissemination of ideas and information. In societies where this is prevented by the State, where censorship, etc., applies, they can be expected to be against the State and in favour of individual rights, since their own lack of freedom will induce in them this general posture. But once they have won their own particular rights – the right to say what they want – it cannot be assumed that they will continue to do battle for freedom in general; the freedom, that is, for people to *do* what they want as well as say what they want.

It is deeply important that this point be understood, since it goes to the heart of the contemporary problem of freedom. Individual freedom, let it be bluntly said, is too important a matter to be left to the tender mercies of those who make use of only one aspect of it: writers, philosophers, artists, journalists, academics, etc. The conditions which used to help guarantee their general concern about human freedom, and their general determination to prevent State interference with it, no longer apply, and have not done so in Britain to any significant extent in modern times. Because their particular freedoms have been made safe, they lack that militant, crusading fervour for freedom which is only provoked in an individual, or in a group, that itself is denied freedom.

What has to be recognized, in short, is that the classical group in society which used to be relied upon to articulate and proclaim the general cause of freedom – that is to say, in broad terms, the intellectuals – can no longer be relied upon to do so, except in so far as it is of value to them. About freedom's absolute value in the field of artistic expression, in the media – Press, television, etc. – they are still as dogmatic as ever they were in the past. Censorship is taboo as an article of libertarian faith. Nobody must be prevented from saying or writing what they want to say or write, since intellectuals know in their bones how important freedom is to these activities. This they know from personal experience, sense it every day as they do their various things. The case for freedom in these areas does not need to be made since it makes itself. Writers and artists know it deep down in their very beings, in the same way as believers know the truths of their religion. But they no longer know the case for freedom in a general sense, as it applies to all the other groups in society – manufacturers, financiers, builders, traders, shopkeepers, doctors, workers, etc., all the vast variety of people who want to be free to *do* things rather than say them.

This is a new and wholly alarming development, since intellectuals are the natural, indeed the only, disseminators of ideas, the group in society which obviously does most to set the intellectual climate. So long as they were denied their freedom, and were therefore provoked into a general crusading disposition against the State, the climate which they set was generally libertarian as much on behalf of others as on behalf of themselves; sympathetic to the doers as well as to the thinkers. But contrary to the general assumption, there is nothing inevitable or permanent about such a fortunate state of affairs; nothing inevitable or permanent about the inclination of intellectuals to champion all freedoms, not just their own.

Rather the reverse. It is in the nature of intellectuals, once they are assured of their own liberty, to want to improve society according to some ideal or pattern which the liberties of others interfere with or preclude; to want to encompass ideals in practice that they have thought up in theory. A free society – free, that is for the doers as well as the thinkers – is not at all necessarily congenial to the typical intellectual, who will find it tiresomely muddled and unpredictable, confused and unsatisfactory. While it is perfectly true that intellectuals are the best champions of freedom in circumstances where the State seeks to shackle freedom of expression since, to put it crudely, they have the gift of the gab and the power to persuade and inspire, it is equally true that in other circumstances – where their own interests are not involved – they may be the worst defenders of all, being more tempted than most to see in the State a perfect instrument to impose the ideal patterns of their choice; and more skilled than most in dressing up such a use of authority with fine sentiments and beguiling justifications; putting, that is, the best face on it.

This surely is what has been happening in Britain in recent years. It would be fair to say that the great majority of the intellectual community show very little concern about encroachments on individual freedom by the State, except where and when they trespass on the still sacred rights of free expression. The classical liberal case for freedom in most of the innumerable areas of human activity – business, trade, building, medicine, education, manufacture, agriculture, etc. – is scarcely ever heard. Governments in all these areas can and do extend the scope and scale of their control and interference, in ways blatantly and brazenly at variance with classical liberal principles, without the intellectual community raising many peeps of protest. Indeed, more likely than not, the intellectual community will be actively promoting and supporting such uses of State power. But only let a Minister seek to regulate what, say, goes into a newspaper, or issue some direction to a publisher, then and only then will the case for freedom be heard resounding throughout the land.

As a result, a whole generation has grown up in an intellectual climate highly discouraging to a proper understanding of the case for freedom; perhaps even uniquely discouraging, and discouraging in a peculiarly debilitating way. For what we have now is an intellectual community careless about freedom in general, since its own particular freedoms are secure enough. And because the intellectual community is not provoked into writing and thinking about liberty, the status and standing of this great ideal has sensationally declined, since those who are still concerned about it – the doers – are precisely those who lack the verbal skills to make their concern persuasive or dominant in the public mind. In a sense, therefore, the inviolability of the one freedom – freedom of expression – has tended to endanger all other freedoms, by inducing in those who should be the intellectual guardians of freedom a complacent lack of concern about it, which in turn infects the whole climate of opinion. Not for many centuries, therefore, has there been so little understanding of what freedom is really about, the principles on which it rests, the values that it serves, and the dangers to civilization that flow from its absence, precisely because those who used to illuminate these truths no longer feel the need to do so, and those who do feel the need to do so are not the people who have the public ear.

I have thought it useful to describe this state of affairs before even mentioning the name of the subject of this essay, since in my view his importance cannot be understood or appreciated unless seen against this particular background. For F. A. Hayek, the Nobel prize-winning political economist, is remarkable, even magnificent, largely in relation to his time: as an expositor of the principles of freedom – in a classic work, *The Constitution of Liberty – during a period when no other first-class thinker saw fit to treat this theme on such a scale*; still less to devote this life to its elaboration and elucidation in book after book, lecture after lecture, pamphlet after pamphlet, the whole oeuvre constituting the fullest and finest defence of freedom written in this dark century. And in large measure it is not primarily a defence of the freedom of expression – which needs no defence, since none in the West really dare attack it, at least intellectually – but a defence of the doers, for whom no other comparable intellectual giant has seen fit to speak.

But how strangely and sadly few in Britain have ever heard of him, let alone read him. His only moment of popular attention – which earned him more notoriety than fame – came towards the end of the second world war with the publication of *The Road to Serfdom*, which strongly argued the case against socialism in terms easily understandable to the general public. Winston Churchill, in his notorious Gestapo broadcast during the 1945 general election, drew on it very heavily in an attempt to convince voters that the logical end of the socialist road was the concentration camp. Needless to say this was a political blunder of the first order, since the then Labour Party under the leadership of Clement Attlee – who had been Churchill's deputy throughout the war against Hitler – did not seem at all likely to lead the British people towards a condition of serfdom. What nonsense to pretend that mild Mr Attlee's kind of socialism, that is to say, the British kind of democratic socialism, could be inimical to freedom. Only an émigré German professor like Hayek could write such nonsense.

Thus it came to pass that this great writer was written off in Britain as a kind of continental crank, who knew nothing about Britain, an impression which gained ground throughout the whole period of the first postwar Labour Government which, to most people, did not seem to be moving towards a police state in any way recognizable to the man in the street. This was a period when the face of socialism seemed eminently benign and gentle, bent on good works, i.e. building up a Welfare State. Nationalization, it is true, was not an economic success, did not seem to be working in a practical sense. But its disappointing practical results did not seem to be confirming Hayek's prophetic warnings about socialism as the path to serfdom; to bankruptcy perhaps, but not to serfdom.

Increasingly, therefore, the argument about socialism was reduced to a non-ideological level, with public opinion, in the fifties, swinging back towards a preference for private enterprise, not because such a system was more free but because it seemed better able to deliver the goods. The question, it seemed, was not theoretical but practical. Free enterprise worked; socialism did not. Why bother with a lot of theory, and arguments about principle, when the case for capitalism, and against socialism, could be made so much better in terms of economic growth. 'You have never had it so good.' That was the simple, eloquent case for capitalism, which did not need a Hayek to make.

But how different the problem is today, when neither socialism nor capitalism seem to work, in the sense of delivering the goods. It is a period, manifestly, of great uncertainty. Individuals do not know what to do; nor do governments. But something has to be done, since crisis threatens. It is precisely at such moments in history that principles do matter, since the temptation to ignore them is so great. Principle is the only anchor against panic; the only anchor that prevents the ship of State being swept from its moorings out into an open sea of pragmatic experimentation leading God knows where. The last period of panic was in the late twenties and early thirties, when the great slump struck. But that was a period, at least in Britain and the United States, when the great body of the people were still rooted in the principles of a free society; deeply impregnated in its values and assumptions and modes of thought, to an extent that may even have placed too many limitations on pragmatic State experimentation, at any rate in the field of economic management. The anchor may possibly have been too heavy. (Not perhaps for Roosevelt in the United States, but certainly for the British National Government of Ramsay Macdonald.)

But what anchors of principle exist today? It surely has to be recognized that the ship of State is infinitely less firmly moored to the principles of a free society than it was then. Social justice, equality, these are the contemporary anchors. Whatever pragmatic solutions are found for this economic crisis, they will tend to be within the confines of these ideals – rather than that of liberty – which means, in practice, that the interests of organized labour will be protected at all costs, and the rights of private property sacrificed, and the power of the State enhanced in all respects except those that interfere with the power of organized labour.

This, as I say, is likely to be the general direction, since in the absence of any widespread understanding of the principles of a free society, there will be no countervailing anchor holding back the ship of State; no body of opinion weighty enough, solid enough, to act as such an anchor. This, let it be said, was precisely the eventuality against which Hayek warned, and which his works were written to prevent. Almost single-handedly he has, since the war, sought to spread the doctrine of freedom in a thoroughly un-British way, demonstrating the need for it to be understood as a whole, and defended as a whole, since to abandon one stronghold was to endanger the entire front. 'Doctrinaire', that was the accusation levelled against him by pragmatic conservatives, anxious to steal the socialist clothes. But that was in the days of Conservative power, when doctrine seemed unnecessary.

Today it is a very different story. The writings of Hayek are returning to favour in Tory circles, with Mrs Thatcher and Sir Keith Joseph using them for bedside reading. It is the same in the United States, where he is fast being elevated into a cult hero by

Republican politicians in desperate need of intellectual ballast. The reason is very clear. Of all the outstanding political philosophers writing in the postwar era, he has most consistently, most bravely, and most powerfully, championed the cause of a free society, not only in relation to those parts of it which every intellectual can cherish – freedom of expression – or those parts of it which are obvious to all – freedom from arbitrary arrest, imprisonment, etc. – but also those parts, like the freedom not to join a trade union, or the freedom not to be taxed for reasons of State social engineering, or freedom in education, medicine, or the freedom to trade, manufacture, do business, make money, which are now out of fashion and for which relatively few now see the need. It is the comprehensiveness of his understanding of the principle of freedom, his awareness of the need to defend it across the board, and of the logical impossibility of not accepting the disadvantages of freedom if the supreme advantages are not to be endangered, that gives his writing such supreme contemporary relevance. Anchors need to be made of iron: ponderous, heavy, inflexible, inelegant. In calm waters it is tempting to ignore their value. But when the wind begins to rise and the sea grows turbulent, no ship can do without them for long. It is in that sense that the writings of Hayek today are indispensable, and increasingly recognized as such by those concerned with freedom.

Yet they have one flaw. One reads *The Constitution of Liberty* from cover to cover – and I know of no more satisfying and stimulating exercise – without coming across a single reference to what seems to me the main obstacle to a free society in present conditions, at least in Britain: the hard facts of political and economic *power*. The most powerful body in the country, the trade unions, are not interested in individual freedom. This is not all that surprising. Trade unions come into existence because workers recognized that, as individuals, they could not prosper in a free and competitive society, since they lacked the gifts to make good on their own. Quite realistically, they saw that their best chance of acquiring bargaining power was by being organized into a mass, the strength of which would depend on solidarity, disciplined uniformity, sticking together, acting as one. Weak as individuals, their instinct was to combine, as a result of which they became strong as a group; eventually more than strong, since in a modern technologically-interdependent economy they are virtually invincible. But their strength depended, and still depends, on acting as a mass, on each individual worker staying in line, sacrificing his own individual freedom of action for the general good. Nothing necessarily wrong with that. In many ways the spirit of comradeship it inspires has much to commend it. But a powerful group whose strength depends on its members acting uniformly is scarcely likely to be very interested in the principles of individual freedom.

The trade unions today, however, are the dominant group in society, to all intents and purposes the new ruling class, whose values, ways of thinking, and traditions help determine the whole political culture, just as bourgeois values and modes of thought helped to form the political culture of the nineteenth century. But unlike the nineteenth century bourgeoisie which understood and appreciated individual freedom, its members being, par excellence, able to make use of it, do well out of it – material interest therefore buttressing political principle – the twentieth century trade union has no such understanding and appreciation, since its members, by definition, are those acutely conscious of their inability to make use of individual freedom and also acutely conscious of the extent to which their material interest depends on its denial.

This new problem does not seem to me adequately dealt with in Hayek's great work. His solution is simply to bring the trade unions under the law, so as to deprive them of the power to destroy a free society. But how is a Government to be strong enough to do so in a democracy, where the trade unions are so strong as to be uncoerceable, unless it takes emergency powers, calls in the army, etc., none of which are exactly liberal measures or ones that come easily to a Government made up of liberal-minded people, trying to maintain the votes of a liberal-minded electorate.

Ever since the 1914–18 war, when the potential power of the trade unions was first properly perceived in this country, it has been one of the main Conservative Party aims to fudge this issue by a series of political and economic compromises, designed to outwit the Labour movement. But this has meant doing what Hayek deplores: abandoning liberal principles all along the line, stealing socialist clothes, acting pragmatically, becoming, at times, almost as collectivist as the Labour Party. But what else can be done, realistically speaking, in a society where the dominant economic group is a mass movement uninterested in individual freedom; indeed, because of its history and traditions, positively inimical to it?

I suspect that Hayek does not have the answer to this problem; that this giant is as baffled by it as all the rest of us pygmies. Until it is found, the marvellous intellectual edifice which he has constructed to house the principles of a free society, so seemingly solid and spacious and beautiful to behold, will lack a roof. That is Professor Hayek's next task, which really would be a crowning achievement.

THE SUBJECTS – AND SOME OF THEIR WORKS

ADAM SMITH

The Theory of Moral Sentiments.
An Inquiry into the Nature and Causes of the Wealth of Nations.
Essays on Philosophical Subjects.
Lectures on Justice, Police, Revenue and Arms; delivered in the University of Glasgow.

JOHN STUART MILL

Essays on Some Unsettled Questions of Political Economy.
Principles of Political Economy.
Enfranchisement of Women.
On Liberty.
Thoughts on Parliamentary Reform.
Dissertations and Discussions; Political, Philosophical and Historical.
Considerations on Representative Government.
An Examination of Sir William Hamilton's Philosophy.
England and Ireland.
The Subjection of Women.
Autobiography.
Nature, The Unity of Religion and Theism.
Socialism.
Utilitarianism, Liberty, and Representative Government.
On Social Freedom.
Mill on Bentham and Coleridge.

ALFRED MARSHALL

The Economics of Industry (with Mary Paley Marshall).
Principles of Economics.

Elements of Economics and Industry.
Industry and Trade.
Money, Credit and Commerce.
Official Papers.

JOHN MAYNARD KEYNES

Indian Currency and Finance.
The Economic Consequences of the Peace.
A Treatise on Probability.
A Revision of the Treaty.
The Economic Consequences of Mr. Churchill.
A Tract on Monetary Reform.
A Short View of Russia.
The End of Laissez-Faire.
A Treatise on Money.
Essays in Persuasion.
The Means to Prosperity.
Essays in Biography.
The General Theory of Employment, Interest, and Money.
How to Pay for the War.
Two Memoirs: Dr Melchior: A Defeated Enemy, and My Early Beliefs.

LUDWIG VON MISES

Socialism – An Economic and Sociological Analysis.
The Theory of Money and Credit.
Bureaucracy.
Omnipotent Government – The Rise of the Total State and Total War.
Human Action – A Treatise on Economics.
Planning for Freedom.
The Anti-Capitalistic Mentality.
Free and Prosperous Commonwealth.

MILTON FRIEDMAN

Income from Independent Professional Practice.
Essays in Positive Economics.
A Theory of Consumption Function.
A Program for Monetary Stability.
Capitalism and Freedom.
Price Theory; A Provisional Text.
A Monetary History of the United States 1867–1960 (with Ann Jacobson Schwartz).
Inflation: Causes and Consequences.
The Balance of Payments: Free vs Flexible Exchange Rates (with Robert U. Roosa).
Dollars and Deficits.
Optimum Quantity of Money and Other Essays.
Monetary vs Fiscal Policy (with Walter H. Heller).
Monetary Statistics of the United States (with Ann Jacobson Schwartz).
A Theoretical Framework for Monetary Analysis.
Counter-Revolution in Monetary Theory.
Money and Economic Development.
There's No Such Thing as a Free Lunch.

SIR KARL POPPER

The Open Society and Its Enemies.
The Poverty of Historicism.
The Logic of Scientific Discovery.
Conjectures and Refutations.

F. A. HAYEK

Prices and Production.
Monetary Theory and the Trade Cycle.
Monetary Nationalism and International Stability.
Collectivist Economic Planning.
Profits, Interest, and Investment.

The Pure Theory of Capital.
The Road to Serfdom.
Individualism and Economic Order.
John Stuart Mill and Harriet Taylor: Their Friendship and Subsequent Marriage.
The Counter-Revolution of Science.
The Sensory Order.
Capitalism and the Historians.
The Constitution of Liberty.
Studies in Philosophy, Politics and Economics.
Law, Legislation and Liberty.

**Roads to Freedom, Essays in Honour of Friedrich A. von Hayek*

THE AUTHORS

ANTONY FLEW

Antony Flew is Professor of Philosophy at the University of Reading. He was an Exhibitioner and Casberd Scholar of St John's College, Oxford, and took a first class honours degree in Greats. He then lectured in Philosophy at Christ Church, Oxford, and from 1950 to 1954 in Moral Philosophy at the University of Aberdeen. From October, 1954, to December, 1971, he was Professor of Philosophy at the University of Keele. He has held many temporary overseas teaching appointments including that of Professor of Philosophy at the University of Calgary, Canada.

His books include *Hume's Philosophy of Belief*; *God and Philosophy*; *Evolutionary Ethics*; *An Introduction to Western Philosophy*; and *Thinking about Thinking*. He has edited *Logic and Language*; *New Essays in Philosophical Theology*; *Essays in Conceptual Analysis*; *Malthus – An Essay on the Principle of Population*. His book *Crime or Disease?* was published by Macmillan early in 1973.

MALCOLM HOPPE

Malcolm Hoppe is an economist and is responsible for research on government and business. He was formerly a political correspondent. In recent years he has won prominence as an expert on local government finance and is the author of several studies on local government and the economics of direct labour building. His studies include *Direct Labour and the Rates, What Went Wrong?*; *The Swing from Direct Labour*; *Death of a Doctrine*; *The Sad Story of Direct Labour Building Maintenance*; *Direct Labour – What Councillors Need to Know*.

A. R. ILERSIC

A. R. Ilersic has been Professor of Social Studies at Bedford College, University of London, since 1966. He is author of *Government Finance and Fiscal Policy in Post-War Britain* and *The Taxation of Capital Gains*. He is also U.K. Correspondent to the Canadian

Tax Foundation and is author of the 1969–74 scheme of rate equalization in Greater London.

MICHAEL IVENS

Michael Ivens is Director of Aims of Industry. He is the author and editor of a number of books on politics, economics and industry. They include *The Case for Capitalism*; *Which Way? 13 Dialogues on Choices Facing Britain*; *Industry and Values*; *The Practice of Industrial Communication: Case Studies in Management*. He is also Director of the Foundation for Business Responsibilities, and was formerly vice-president of the Junior Hospital Doctors' Association and Director of the Working Together Campaign. He has held a number of senior appointments in business, including the oil, telecommunications and engineering industries, and is author of a number of books of poetry. He was for six years joint-editor of *Twentieth Century*.

MICHAEL JEFFERSON

Michael Jefferson is Head of Economic Environment in one of the world's largest oil companies. He has been manager of an economic consultancy and Deputy Director of the Industrial Policy Group. He is author of articles, signed papers and contributions to books which reflect his interest not only in applied economics but in the history of economic thought, social history and nineteenth-century fiction, and the mass media.

WILFRID SENDALL

Wilfrid Sendall took a history degree at Magdalen College, Oxford, and since then has had a distinguished career as political correspondent extending over more than forty years, only interrupted by five years in the Royal Marines during the second world war. He has been in turn chief political correspondent of the *Daily Telegraph*, *Sunday Express*, *News of the World* and *Daily Express*. Nowadays he is a freelance political writer.

ALFRED SHERMAN

Alfred Sherman is a graduate of the London School of Economics, journalist, economic analyst, and public affairs consultant. He has written several studies of the border line between politics and economics, and broadcasts on Communist bloc affairs. He has contributed essays to economic, political and sociological reviews. His writings include "Nationalism and Communists in the Arab World: a Reappraisal", in *The Middle East in Transition*, ed, W. Z. Laqueur, Routledge, 1958; "Tito, the Reluctant Revisionist". in *Revisionism*, ed. L. Labedz, Allen and Unwin, 1961; "Immigration in the Deptford Election, 1964", in *Colour and the British Electorate, 1964* ed. N. Deakin, Pall Mall, 1965; "Our Complacent Satirists", in *Encounter*, June, 1963; "Capitalism and Liberty", in *The Case for Capitalism*, Michael Joseph and Aims of Industry, 1967; *Councillors, Councils and Public Relations* (Barry Rose). He is a member of a London borough council, and has written a number of studies on local government problems for Aims of Industry and the Churchill Press. Currently he is working with Sir Keith Joseph at the Centre for Policy Studies.

A. A. WALTERS

A. A. Walters is Cassel Professor of Economics (with special reference to money and banking) in the University of London at London School of Economics. After graduating from University College, Leicester, he carried out research at Nuffield College, Oxford, before joining the faculty of the University of Birmingham, where in 1961 he became professor and head of the Department of Econometrics and Social Statistics.

He has been visiting professor of a number of United States universities, and his consultancies include governments and international institutions. He has served on several official panels, including the Roskill Commission on the third London Airport.

Professor Walters was until 1971 joint managing editor of the *Review of Economic Studies* and is a member of the editorial board of the *Journal of Urban Economics* and the *Journal of Money Credit and Banking*. He is a prolific writer of articles, which appear all over the world on money and banking, transport, production costs and prices, social accounting, and other business and economic subjects. He has written or collaborated in a number of books and monographs. They include a textbook, *An Introduction to Econometrics* (Macmillan) and a Penguin, *Money and Banking*. He wrote *The Politicisation of Economic Decisions* and *Money and Inflation* for Aims of Industry.

PEREGRINE WORSTHORNE

Peregrine Worsthorne, deputy editor and feature writer of *The Sunday Telegraph*, went to Magdalen College, Oxford, and Peterhouse, Cambridge, after Stowe School. He was with the *Glasgow Herald* before joining *The Times* in 1948, and was *Times* correspondent in Washington 1950–52. In 1955 he joined *The Daily Telegraph* as leader writer, travelling extensively in the USA, Western Europe and Africa before becoming assistant editor of *The Sunday Telegraph* in 1961 and deputy editor next year. He frequently appears on public affairs programmes on television and radio, and has contributed to a number of periodicals, including *Encounter*, *New York Times*, *Foreign Affairs*, *Washington Post*, *Spectator*, *Time and Tide*. Mr Worsthorne edits the *International Review*. He is author of *The Socialist Myth* (Cassell).